STANDARD GRADE
Music
course notes

✕ John Montgomery ✕

Text © 2002 John Montgomery
Design and layout © 2002 Leckie & Leckie Ltd
Cover image © Comstock

3rd edition, reprinted 2005

ISBN 1-898890-21-8

Published by
Leckie & Leckie Ltd, 8 Whitehill Terrace, St. Andrews, Scotland, KY16 8RN
tel. 01334 475656   fax. 01334 477392
enquiries@leckieandleckie.co.uk   www.leckieandleckie.co.uk

Edited by
Ross Allan

Special thanks to
Brian Carty, Bob Dewar, Alison Irving, Carolynn McIntyre (former Principal Teacher of Music, Drummond Community High School), Kathryn McPhee (Principal Teacher of Music, Currie Community High School) and Caleb Rutherford (cover design)

A CIP Catalogue record for this book is available from the British Library.

Leckie & Leckie Ltd is a division of Granada Learning Limited, part of ITV plc.

CONTENTS

INTRODUCTION

The Elements

Standard Grade Music is a two-year course in which you will look at four different elements of study:

- **Solo Performing**
- **Group Performing**
- **Inventing**
- **Listening**

This Book and CD

This book and CD are about these four elements. They will help you both in the classroom and at home in understanding what is required to successfully complete the course.

The book is divided into Performing, Inventing and Listening. Key concepts you should know are highlighted **in blue** throughout the text in this book. You will also find concise definitions of these concepts in the Glossary on pages 73 to 78.

The CD is designed to be used as you work through the book. It has ideas for inventing and extracts of varying styles of music. A list of the 30 tracks on the CD is given on pages 79 and 80.

Assessment

On your Standard Grade Music certificate you will be awarded a separate result for each of the four elements. The combination of these results will give you an overall grade.

Solo Performing is assessed by a visiting examiner. You will play a short programme of pieces on your solo instrument to an examiner near the end of your course.

Group Performing is assessed by your teacher throughout your course. You will perform on your group instrument with other players. A final result will be decided by your teacher towards the end of your course.

Inventing is also assessed by your teacher throughout your course. You will invent music of your own choice. Final marks are decided by your teacher towards the end of your course.

Listening is assessed in an exam at the end of your course. The listening exam contains mainly multiple-choice questions, using taped extracts of music.

PERFORMING

Solo Performing

During your Standard Grade Course you will play contrasting styles of music in preparation for the performance that you will give near the end of your course.

What you are aiming for

This live performance of 4–6 minutes will take place in front of a visiting examiner who will come to your school in February or March of your fourth year. The standard of pieces you play and how well you play them will determine which grade you will achieve.

Performing with confidence

This is easier said than done! However, there are steps you can take to help control those nerves. The most obvious one is *be prepared*.

It is good to be a bit nervous. Most good performers feel butterflies in the stomach. You will think more quickly and react swiftly but the difficult bit is keeping it all under control!

Points to remember

1. **Get into the routine of regular practice – this will pay off at exam time. Not doing enough during the course and then having a great flurry of activity just before the big day doesn't work.**

2. **Try to record your pieces. This is very important not only as an accurate record of your work but also gives you the opportunity to listen to yourself. We are often too busy playing a piece to listen carefully. You'll be amazed at the things you'll hear. This is often a very good way of finding and correcting mistakes, e.g. unexplained changes in speed!**

3. **Practise playing your pieces to your friends and relatives – this will give you confidence – and your audience will (hopefully) enjoy it!**

4. **When you go into the exam, remind yourself how hard you have worked over the last couple of years. Relax, and decide that the examiner is going to enjoy your performance. A smile and a 'hello' will help put you at your ease.**

5. **Take your time and make sure you are happy with the set up: for example, can you see the accompanist? Check the examiner can see you clearly. Sort out these matters with your teacher before the exam to increase your confidence and improve your performance.**

6. During your exam you may make a few small mistakes. Do not worry if this happens. Every performer makes mistakes no matter how good they are. Though your playing has to be accurate in every way, your mark will be based on your overall interpretation of the music (how well you have expressed the music).

7. Although you will be a bit nervous, remember that the examiner wants you to do your best, and knows how you will be feeling. Most examiners are also music teachers and they will put you at your ease. Remember that they will be trying to pass you and give you the best possible result.

8. If you are playing an electronic keyboard (or other instrument which has settings), make sure you are organised in advance and that you are completely familiar with its settings and operations.

9. If your exam is in the morning, get up early – especially if you are singing or blowing.

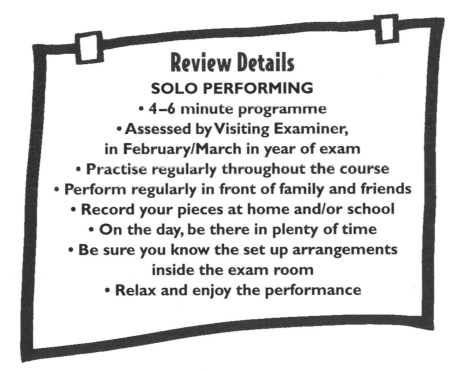

Review Details
SOLO PERFORMING
- 4–6 minute programme
- Assessed by Visiting Examiner, in February/March in year of exam
- Practise regularly throughout the course
- Perform regularly in front of family and friends
- Record your pieces at home and/or school
- On the day, be there in plenty of time
- Be sure you know the set up arrangements inside the exam room
- Relax and enjoy the performance

Group Performing

Playing in a group is a very important and enjoyable part of music making. Remember that playing your group instrument is just as important as playing your solo instrument. During your course you will have opportunities to play in different instrumental groups.

You will be assessed on how well you can play your group instrument and how your playing fits in with other musicians. Your teacher will record your progress in group performing throughout your two-year course. This is called continuous assessment.

Points to remember

1. **In your group work you will play various pieces of music. A 'group' can be as few as two players, so long as they are both pupils from your Standard Grade class. There should be no more than eight players in your ensemble.**

2. **Extra rehearsal time may be needed. Difficulties with instruments or music may occur. It is important that you are sensitive and helpful to the needs of others in your music group. Carefully plan the way you use your rehearsal and recording time.**

3. **When recording your performances it is very important that your part can be clearly heard. No one else should be playing the same part as you. Make sure the microphone is nearest you, even though this may mean that the recording will sound unbalanced. It's up to you to produce a good record of your work on tape.**

4. **You may also have opportunities at home to record with friends but be sure to mark your tape carefully, announcing on your tape the title and part you are playing.**

5. **As well as your tape, have copies of the music you are performing.**

6. **Make sure you have enough recordings to justify the level you hope to achieve. Your result in Group Performing will be based upon the best work you produce during your course.**

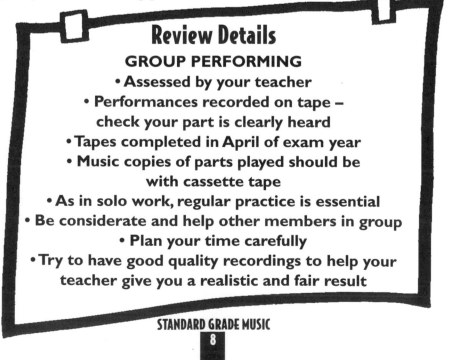

Review Details
GROUP PERFORMING
- **Assessed by your teacher**
- **Performances recorded on tape – check your part is clearly heard**
- **Tapes completed in April of exam year**
- **Music copies of parts played should be with cassette tape**
- **As in solo work, regular practice is essential**
- **Be considerate and help other members in group**
- **Plan your time carefully**
- **Try to have good quality recordings to help your teacher give you a realistic and fair result**

INVENTING

Introduction

One of the most exciting areas of Standard Grade Music is the Inventing element. The three activities in this element are:

- **Arranging**

- **Composing**

- **Improvising**

These all mean creating **something new**, something which is new to you – the inventor.

Arranging means altering a piece of music in such a way as to add something new and original to it (e.g. change the speed, the instruments used or the style).

Composing means creating a completely new piece of music (e.g. a song, a piece for a group of instruments, or a soundscape).

Improvising means making-up music spontaneously ('on the spot'). The most common way to improvise is to create melody over a given set of chords.

During your course you build up a folio of inventions, recording them on cassette tape. You will have more than one which represent your best work. Your teacher carries out the assessment of your inventing throughout your two-year course.

What's inventing all about?

Think of inventing music as something which is *natural* for us all to do – because it is! When someone asks you to draw a face for example, you do not consider whether you can or not – you can. You are asked to give this face a large nose and tiny eyes, and a pimple on the cheek – no problem. Now you are given a big paint box and brush. Give your face a black moustache, bright red lips and a blue hat. Wrap a long striped scarf around the neck. You've done exactly as you were asked. Is it good? Well, maybe. It might be better next time you try.

Someone else asks you to write down exactly what happened in your life yesterday: all the details of where you went, who you spoke to, what time you went to bed, etc... Now you are asked to change some of these details. Invent a place you would have liked to have gone to. What amazing person did you meet? You landed up in a yellow taxi in New York – it's snowing hard – a man with a gun breaks into your taxi as you stop at the lights on 5th Avenue. All you can remember is that he has a moustache and is wearing a long striped scarf! How good is your story? Maybe great and maybe not. However, you have created it. It has shape and direction: it starts, it ends and so on.

Inventing music is just like this, whether it be improvising, composing or arranging. You are going to say something new and refreshing and you don't have to be Beethoven or The Beatles.

You may already be a budding young composer – or this may be your first attempt. Whatever, everyone can create something new. Don't panic – the ideas will come.

Once you have learned how to create ideas and place them within a simple structure you can explore and enjoy your inventing – as well as receiving a good final result for your trouble!

The starting point

A stimulus is the starting point of an invention: it is 'the spur', 'the spark', 'the first idea'.

Here are some examples of a stimulus:

A poem about a train journey What instruments could represent the rhythm of the train? What scenes go by the train window? How could you describe them in sound? Would the piece start slowly? How would you construct your music? How would you represent the power of the train?

The inside of a large clock Each part moves and repeats perfectly. With all these moving parts, would you want to have several different types of sounds or instruments playing? Would each instrument play the same pattern of notes over and over?

Film of a new space exploration What effects could you use to represent the spacecraft? How do you time your music accurately with a given video sequence? Did something go terribly wrong on this mission? Would long sustained sounds or short staccato notes represent the flight into space?

Arranging a keyboard piece You suspect the keyboard melody you have been playing would sound great on a clarinet, with the bass guitar playing a new rhythm line. You think the piece would sound better at a slower speed giving it a different emotional feel. How could you write this down for the other players?

A seascape You have chosen a chord progression to improvise over. What effect could you use to represent the gentle swell of the ocean? Trills, with gradual changes in volume? Long notes to represent the calm? Staccato notes with chromatic runs as the weather changes?

These are a few suggestions you may wish to return to and use as a stimulus for a future invention. There are endless other stimuli. Always ask yourself questions when you have decided on an idea: what form will my piece take; what instruments are available to me and who is going to play them; what effect do I want to create?

The answers to these questions will probably change during the course of your inventing. Don't worry! It's a healthy sign that your ideas and thoughts are evolving, changing and progressing.

Six inventing frameworks

It is essential to use a framework (structure) around which to create your musical inventions. Here are six different frameworks for inventing music with examples of each on the CD:

1. **Pentatonic**

2. **Blues**

3. **Arrange**

4. **Ostinato**

5. **Improvise**

6. **Words**

1. Pentatonic

The **pentatonic scale**, or five-note scale, has been in existence for many centuries. Civilisations from China to Africa and India to Scotland have based melodies upon it. Unlike the **major** and **minor** scales, the pentatonic scale usually has no **semitones**.

The pentatonic scale has been used to create compositions all over the world. Elements within these compositions (such as rhythm, harmony, tempo and instruments used) help us to recognise where the compositions come from.

For instance, if you wanted to create a Chinese-sounding melody, you would have to think carefully about what type of instrumental sound you would use: possibly a harp-like plucking sound or a haunting whistle where you might slide or bend the notes to create a Far-Eastern effect. You may discover these sounds on a guitar, a keyboard or a recorder. Experiment with several different instruments and objects – you'll be amazed at the unlikely sources you will find for the effect you want to create. Or maybe you want to write a melody with a convincing Scottish flavour. Will it be a fast-moving **jig** with triplets, or a slow **waltz**? You may wish to include **Scotch snaps** as part of your rhythm pattern.

If you have access to a keyboard, play the five different black notes **ascending** and **descending**. This is a pentatonic scale no matter which note you start on. Now try playing them in any order to make a simple tune. No matter which order, with some simple rhythm you should end up with a pleasing melody.

To keep things simple, let's make our first note C as in the diagram below and call it note 1.

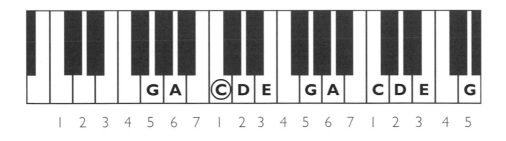

Now you are going to add notes 2, 3, 5 and 6 to make a pentatonic scale.

You can also use the same notes in a different **octave** above or below, to add interest as in the diagram above.

Phrases

When you create melody, try to think of it in phrases just as words are grouped together, for example:

  Question: 'How are you today?'

  Answer: 'I'm very well thank you'.

Groups of notes make a phrase (statement), and, as in the spoken or written word, there is often a question/answer relationship between the phrases. Here are two examples of question and answer musical phrases:

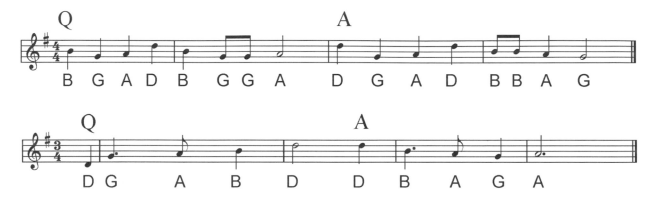

Think too about the *shape* of your melody. How many bars will it have and how many beats will be in each bar? It is common to have eight or sixteen bars to give you a simple and balanced structure.

Each of your phrases could be made up of two bars: two bars for the question and two bars for the answer. Repeating phrases help to strengthen the melody and give it continuity.

Accompanying your melody

Once you have created the phrases, try accompanying your pentatonic melody with simple chords.

Use chords on the keyboard, guitar or piano or have a friend play along with you. Start your melody on a C, an E or a G and make your first chord C. Using the notes C, D, E, G and A try to fit in the following chords as an accompaniment:

Chord of C

Chord of F

Chord of G

You will soon hear that the notes C, E and G in the melody 'fit' the chord of C. Now see which notes fit the chord of F, remembering to avoid using the note F in your melody.

Start your piece with the chord of C, and experiment using the chords of F and G against the pentatonic melody you have created. Finish your piece using the chord of C.

Obviously notes and chords with the same name will work together. Experiment until you like what you hear.

Record your piece on tape and write down its note names. For help with writing your piece down using notation, turn to *Writing it down* on page 45.

Here is an example of a pentatonic melody. See if you can play it and compare it with your own invention. Notice that it follows the pattern of 'question and answer' phrases.

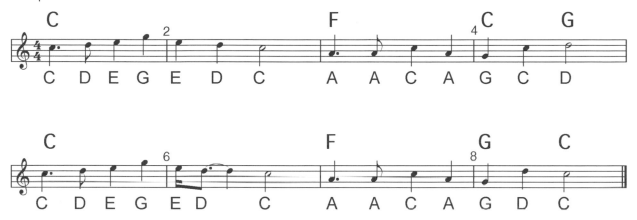

Only the notes of C, D, E, G and A have been used, as this pentatonic tune suggests the key of C. We have also used the chords of I, IV and V (in this case C, F and G). The chords of I, IV and V are called primary chords. They are the most common combination of chords used for accompaniment in all music, no matter what the style, and they are often called the 'three-chord trick'.

Because we are in the key of C, we have made C the first chord of the piece.

Rhythm

To suggest a particular 'feel' in your invention you could introduce a 'thumbprint' (a feature) which will make your piece more convincing. *Highland Walk*, being a Scottish tune, has **Scotch snaps** as its thumbprint (e.g. in bar 6).

Use *similar* rhythms throughout your piece to make it sound continuous and connected.

Try to complete your piece in the key of C adding chords to it. Record your piece and try to write it down.

Extension work

Now we are going to extend our melody and give it a middle section. We are also going to add a new chord, the chord of VI. This is a minor chord and is commonly used to add interest and to take us away briefly from our other three chords.

Because *Highland Walk* is in the key of C, this new chord of VI will be A minor which contains the notes of A, C and E. So right away here are three notes you could use in your melody against the chord of A minor.

You will see the piece has a definite form: it is in three distinct sections, called ABA. This a very common shape for music to be in. This ABA layout is called **ternary form**. 'A' is the first section; 'B' is a new or different section; 'A' is a repeat of the first section.

Here then is the complete piece called *Highland Walk* in the key of C. Listen to the piece on your CD and play it on the keyboard or on the instrument of your choice.

CD1 Highland Walk

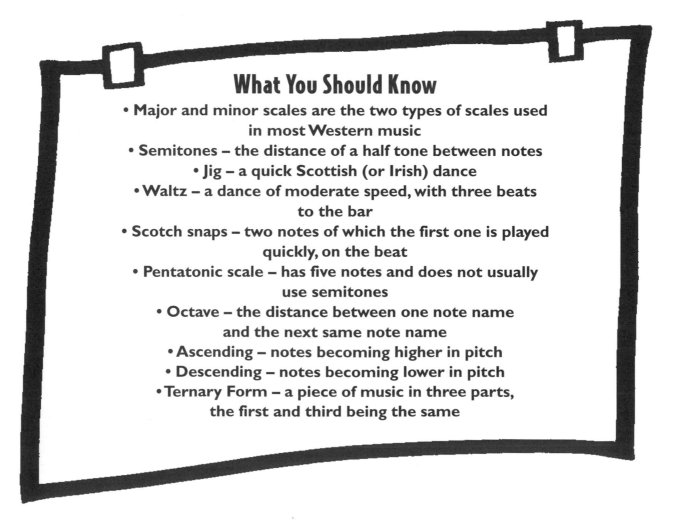

What You Should Know
- **Major and minor scales** are the two types of scales used in most Western music
- **Semitones** – the distance of a half tone between notes
- **Jig** – a quick Scottish (or Irish) dance
- **Waltz** – a dance of moderate speed, with three beats to the bar
- **Scotch snaps** – two notes of which the first one is played quickly, on the beat
- **Pentatonic scale** – has five notes and does not usually use semitones
- **Octave** – the distance between one note name and the next same note name
- **Ascending** – notes becoming higher in pitch
- **Descending** – notes becoming lower in pitch
- **Ternary Form** – a piece of music in three parts, the first and third being the same

HIGHLAND WALK
melody

2. Blues

Blues is an early and very important form of jazz. This style of music had its roots in the terrible misery which black people endured in the eighteenth and nineteenth centuries when millions of them were brought from Africa to the USA and sold as slaves. Conditions were very poor and families were often broken up. Most were sent to work in the cotton fields of the southern states of Louisiana, Alabama and Georgia.

To express their hardship and their hopes for the future they sang spirituals. These songs were originally lines from the Bible, but through time and improvisation their meanings altered.

When black people moved to the big industrial cities, such as Chicago and St Louis, after slavery was abolished in 1865, the Blues became popular throughout the USA. Blues are slow jazz songs often relating to blacks' continuing struggle for equality and basic living and working conditions.

Blue Notes

Using the key of C, here are the notes which make up the Blues scale. The notes of Eb and Bb are called *Blue Notes*. Another blue note often used is F#. Using blue notes gives the music a feel of both major and minor.

C   D   Eb   E   F   F#   G   A   Bb   B   C

Blues Notes (the notes in brackets can also be used)

Blues songs and tunes often use **syncopation** and dotted rhythms in their melody, while the accompaniment remains very straightforward. Try to clap this rhythm. It appears in the Blues song *Carolina Blues* on the CD.

The Twelve-Bar Blues

Blues songs use a particular scale and a simple framework of chords, called the twelve-bar blues.

In the key of C, the **chords** which typically make up a twelve-bar blues are:

C / / / C / / / C / / / C / / /

F / / / F / / / C / / / C / / /

G / / / F / / / C / / / C / / /

Below are slight variations which you could try out:

C / / / F7 / / / C / / / C7 / / /

F / / / F / / / C / / / C / / /

G / / / F7 / / / C / / / C / / /
                     (or G7 when repeating verse)

Using the formula that C = chord I , F = chord IV, and G = chord V you can now change this to any key which suits you.

Using the twelve-bar blues is an exciting way to create a new composition, arrangement or improvisation.

How to start your Blues piece

Line 1. C / / / F / / / C / / / C / / /

Use slow single finger chords or piano/guitar chords as a backing, and try to sing or play a line using the notes of the Blues scale. Make the last note of your melody line longer. It may help you to sing some words along to your melody.

Line 2. F / / / F / / / C / / / C / / /

Use the same melody as for line 1. Don't worry if it doesn't sound good yet. This is the time for trial and error and for experimenting.

Line 3. G / / / F / / / C / / / C / / /

For this line you may want to introduce some new notes that will work with the chord of G. Reintroduce a few notes from your first line to round the melody off. Make sure your last melody note is longer, to make the verse sound complete.

Check again with the Blues scale, especially the blue notes. Have you included any? Write your composition down in any way and worry about the details later. Your teacher will offer you good tips and advice and show you short cuts for putting your ideas down on paper.

Now that you have put a verse or tune together over the given chords, think about an introduction. An introduction sets the speed and mood of the music. An easy introduction is one bar of C chord and one bar of G7 chord.

One other device often used is adding a verse of instrumental melody only. This is called an instrumental or instrumental break and is often an improvisation based on the melody.

Here is the first line of *Carolina Blues*:

See how we have used the blue note Eb against the chord of C. That same note will work well against the F chord in line 2 when the phrase is repeated.

Here are the melody and chords for *Carolina Blues*. Play the music and see how the notes in line 3 complete the verse. The notation is an approximate guide to the CD vocal recording.

Now try putting together your own Blues tune or song. You may find it helpful to write your piece in a different key from that given. Here are the twelve-bar blues chords and blues scales for the keys of G and D.

Twelve-Bar Blues Chords in G

G / / / G / / / G / / / G / / /

C / / / C / / / G / / / G / / /

D / / / C / / / G / / / G / / /

(D7 / / / if repeating)

Blues Scale in G

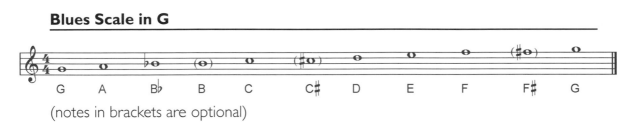

(notes in brackets are optional)

Twelve-Bar Blues Chords in D

D / / / D / / / D / / / D / / /

G / / / G / / / D / / / D / / /

A / / / G / / / D / / / D / / /

(A7 / / / if repeating)

Blues Scale in D

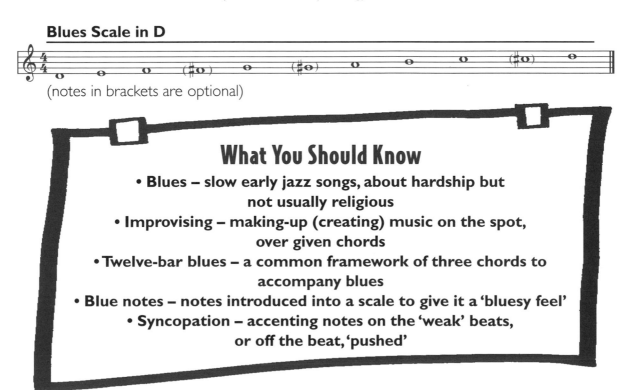

(notes in brackets are optional)

What You Should Know

- **Blues** – slow early jazz songs, about hardship but not usually religious
- **Improvising** – making-up (creating) music on the spot, over given chords
- **Twelve-bar blues** – a common framework of three chords to accompany blues
- **Blue notes** – notes introduced into a scale to give it a 'bluesy feel'
- **Syncopation** – accenting notes on the 'weak' beats, or off the beat, 'pushed'

3. Arrange

Arranging a piece of music means taking music which already exists and *altering* it, usually in a variety of ways, to make it something different – something new.

Which particular piece you choose to arrange should be carefully considered. This will probably be done with the help and guidance of your teacher.

You can give a simple melody a whole new lease of life by changing its:

- **style**
- **key**
- **time signature**
- **speed**
- **instruments**
- **form or shape**
- **melody**
- **harmony**

and you could also **add** to it:

- **counter melody**
- **introduction**
- **new chords**
- **repeats**
- **effects and so on**

You may choose to arrange a TV theme that you like, a favourite pop or folk song or a tune from a book in the keyboard room of your music department for example.

Experiment

As in all inventing, *experimenting* is the key word in arranging. It's good to use your instrument (which includes voice) to try out different ideas.

Imagine that you have chosen the popular Scottish tune *Loch Lomond*.

You know the song, like it, and sang it in class last year. You know roughly what the chords sound like, but have never played them.

You can tell a lot about the piece by looking at the music printed below. What key is it in? How many beats are in the bar? What speed is it played at? Is there an introduction?

Here is the melody line of *Loch Lomond* with note names added below and guitar/keyboard chords above. You could play this melody on most instruments and a friend could play the chords on piano, keyboard or guitar. It has been written in the key of F major.

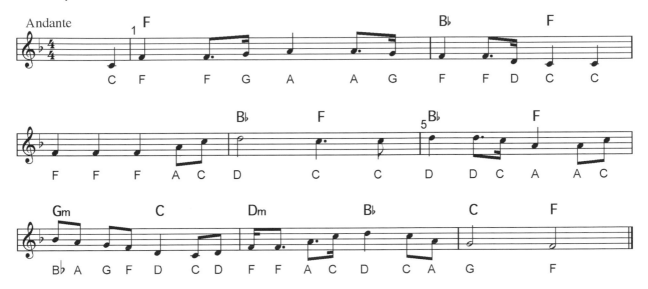

Experiment with tempo, key and changing the number of beats in the bar. Start thinking of where you are going, and what the final product is going to sound like.

Whatever you are arranging, it is important to bear in mind how you are going to produce the final product.

Here is a plan you could follow:

Idea >>>>>>> Develop >>>>>>> Complete

Have you got an idea, a spark, something you thought of as you played a little bit of it?

Idea

You tried playing the first chord with a tinkling effect high up on the keyboard, and immediately the idea of rain came into your head.

You decided to give it a light introduction, based on the chord of F, to represent the rain. You could use a small, bell-like, gentle sound – possibly a small glockenspiel or a metallophone?

Try out a few patterns of notes on the glockenspiel and come up with a simple repeating pattern of notes, e.g.

After hearing snare drum rolls along the corridor, the idea of soldiers crossing the loch in the mist has hit you. You will include the snare at intervals during the piece.

Suddenly the piece is called *Raining on Loch Lomond*.

Develop

Remind yourself of the chords you have used in this tune. You have decided to keep the same chords but move them around a bit so they are now in a different order.

You have tried playing the chords while keeping the same bass note (F). You like the sound this makes and decide to make this feature repeat during the verse. This is called a **pedal bass** (the bass note stays the same, while the chords – the harmony – change).

You experiment with the chord of D minor and decide to include it near the end of the piece.

After playing a little bit of the verse again you decide that it should be a little slower – to create atmosphere.

Now you are going to try making your chord idea work with the tune, and start thinking about the instruments you want to use.

Scribble down your ideas in any way or you'll forget them. Worry about writing it out clearly later. You may even consider making a rough recording at this point.

Complete

You decided to write the chords of C and Bb above the melody you have copied out, with the F bass repeated. Your chords alter towards the end of the tune and you introduce the chord of D minor, having tried this several times to get the right place for it.

A friend has offered to play the melody on the clarinet and your teacher has helped you write the notes. You've got yourself a bass player who loves playing F and you are using the school's best keyboard to play those gently sustained chords. Two other classmates have agreed to play your tuned percussion part – the rain! Your snare drummer is at the ready.

You work on the written parts, remembering your teacher is at hand to help you out with any problems.

Rehearsals towards a recording can begin.

Here is a short example of what it might sound like:

CD3 Raining on Loch Lomond

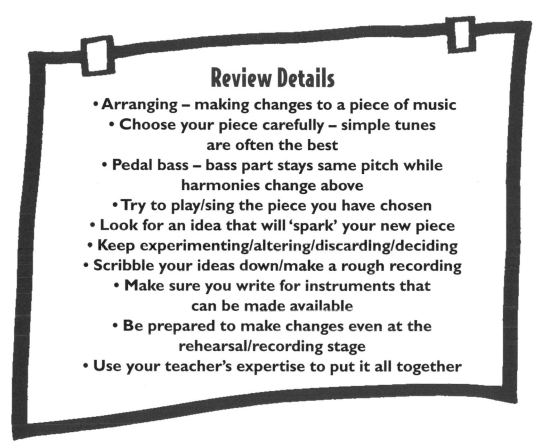

Review Details
- Arranging – making changes to a piece of music
- Choose your piece carefully – simple tunes are often the best
- Pedal bass – bass part stays same pitch while harmonies change above
- Try to play/sing the piece you have chosen
- Look for an idea that will 'spark' your new piece
- Keep experimenting/altering/discarding/deciding
- Scribble your ideas down/make a rough recording
- Make sure you write for instruments that can be made available
- Be prepared to make changes even at the rehearsal/recording stage
- Use your teacher's expertise to put it all together

4. Ostinato

A lot of music is inspired by a story or a poem a composer has read or heard. A poster or painting, a film or newspaper article can spark off the imagination instantly.

In this section we are going to feature a poem and develop a new composition using a musical device called ostinato.

Ostinato is a constantly repeated short melodic phrase or rhythm. It literally means 'obstinate' or 'persistent'.

You can use an ostinato in several different ways. It often represents a repetition (e.g. a machine) or a continuous movement (e.g. the sea). It can be a very effective means of creating atmosphere and tension.

Try to create a simple melodic ostinato. Use only a few notes in your pattern, and keep the notes close together. Build it up by recording your pattern several times and then introducing a new idea above it, with a second ostinato.

Try a rhythmic ostinato on untuned percussion instruments. You could start by creating a simple rhythmic pattern on side drum and introduce the tambourine, the cymbal with brushes, or guiro, using contrasting patterns. This could form the basis of your composition.

Here is a poem by Robert Louis Stevenson:

From A Railway Carriage

Faster than fairies, faster than witches,
Bridges and houses, hedges and ditches;
And charging along like troops in a battle,
All through the meadows the horses and cattle:
All of the sights of the hill and the plain
Fly as thick as driving rain;
And ever again, in the wink of an eye,
Painted stations whistle by.

Here is a child who clambers and scrambles,
All by himself and gathering brambles;
Here is a tramp who stands and gazes;
And there is the green for stringing the daisies!
Here is a cart run away in the road
Lumping along with man and load;
And here is a mill and there is a river:
Each a glimpse and gone for ever!

As you read this poem, you hopefully felt the rhythm of the train as it raced across the countryside. Today's trains still make a pleasing repetitive rhythm as they travel on the track. This is the sort of rhythm that could be referred to as an ostinato.

Read the poem again and see if you could think of a short phrase that could be repeated to represent the train on the tracks.

Try it on a drum. The rhythm of the train could be something like this:

Clap or play this rhythm as you count three in each bar.

Now you are going to add a simple repeating pattern of notes over your rhythm to represent the repetitive motion of the train.

The notes you have chosen suggest a minor key. Remember that the power of an ostinato is often what you add to it. This might be:

1. a further ostinato, gradually building up in layers to represent speed

2. adding a melody

3. changing the harmony while your ostinato continues.

Because the simple pattern of notes you have chosen are in the minor key, you have decided to use minor chords in your accompanying keyboard part. At certain intervals of time your chords will descend gradually and you experiment with different chords against your ostinato.

Look again at the poem. What about the different scenes and objects that rush by? Would you want to represent them in your piece? You could try to introduce the occasional 'characters' as they appear in the poem.

How could the piece start? 'Fairies' and 'witches'? A *flying* sound? Possibly glissando whistles, or trilling flutes diminuendo/crescendo?

'Charging along like troops in a battle' Could a brass instrument, such as a cornet, represent the idea of soldiers?

'Painted stations whistle by' What happens to sound when an object 'whistles by'? The sound gets lower in pitch. What instrument could represent this? Possibly a glissando on the trombone?

'Here is a cart run away in the road' Perhaps a small percussion instrument representing a tin cup rattling against the cart as it bangs down the road?

'Each a glimpse and gone for ever' Does the ostinato of the train on the tracks start to disappear into the distance? (diminuendo)

You can see from these ideas how you can musically develop features from this poem.

Try creating your own piece using some of these ideas. You may find you see the poem quite differently and want to emphasise different lines. Decide on the form of the piece:

1. how it starts

2. what other features appear during the piece

3. how it ends.

It might be wise to have the ostinato playing throughout the piece with parts added or subtracted.

Your choice of instruments is important. Make sure you are using contrasting sounds so that individual parts can be heard.

When writing this piece out you may be able to employ simple signs and drawings for your players, rather than strict notation. You may also be able to direct or conduct the performance live. Here is an example of how your parts could be written:

Here is an example on the CD of the sort of ideas we have suggested on the previous pages:

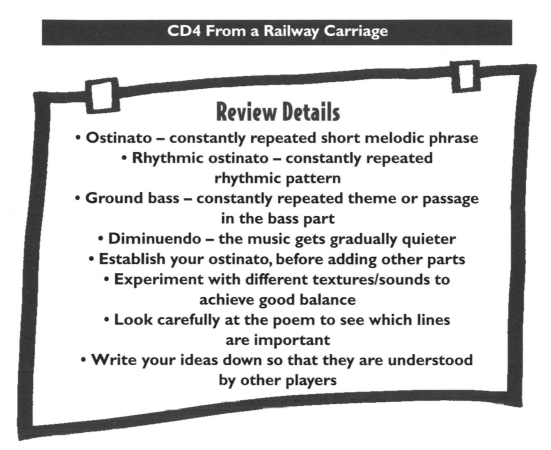

CD4 From a Railway Carriage

Review Details

- **Ostinato – constantly repeated short melodic phrase**
- **Rhythmic ostinato – constantly repeated rhythmic pattern**
- **Ground bass – constantly repeated theme or passage in the bass part**
- **Diminuendo – the music gets gradually quieter**
- **Establish your ostinato, before adding other parts**
- **Experiment with different textures/sounds to achieve good balance**
- **Look carefully at the poem to see which lines are important**
- **Write your ideas down so that they are understood by other players**

5. Improvise

Improvising means creating music 'on the spot'.

Improvising is just about as old as time itself. Long, long ago players would communicate across the land – 'talking' to each other in rhythmic phrases, altering and repeating the patterns and adding variations. This was one of the earliest forms of improvising.

Bach, Mozart and Beethoven were excellent improvisers and gave performances often improvising on their own compositions, by request from their enthralled audiences.

Sadly, improvising has all but died out in Western classical music. Fortunately this is not the case in other cultures such as in India and the Far East, where this form of music-making is very important. It is also not the case as far as jazz, rock and folk music are concerned, where improvising is alive and as popular as ever.

The most common method of improvising is creating melody over given chords. Sometimes in rock and folk songs, you will hear an 'instrumental' improvised on the chords. This has the effect of creating variation to the song. It also gives a player in a group a chance to show off her/his skills and gives a singer an opportunity to improvise around the lyrics.

How to improvise

Individuals improvise in different ways because improvising depends on:

- **the instrument played**

- **the standard played to**

- **the individual's understanding of chords and harmony**

Here are three ways to develop your improvising skills:

1. **clapping rhythms**

2. **playing musical patterns**

3. **adding a melody to given chords**

1. Clapping rhythms

This is a good way to develop your improvising skills. You alter rhythms 'on the spot' to create balanced patterns within a four-beat framework. Try this with a friend. Here are four rhythms. Clap each one and ask your friend to repeat it after you.

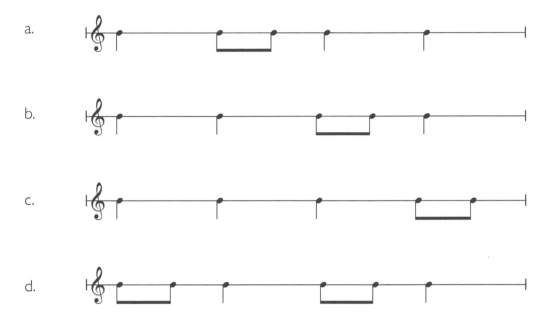

a.

b.

c.

d.

Now let's try to improvise. Ask your friend to clap each rhythm again. 'Answer' the rhythm you hear with a different four-beat rhythm. In your answer, try to use similar rhythms, for example:

These are called 'question and answer' phrases: you're talking to each other without saying a word!

Now try different question and answer rhythms, adding semiquavers (♫) and dotted crotchets with quavers (♩.♪). Keep the beat slow enough so that you can cope with the different rhythms.

2. Playing patterns

This is very similar to clapping rhythms, except you use pitch as well as rhythm. You can do this exercise alone or with a friend. Here are melodies (or 'questions'). First play each melody. Now give an 'answer' to each 'question'. For example:

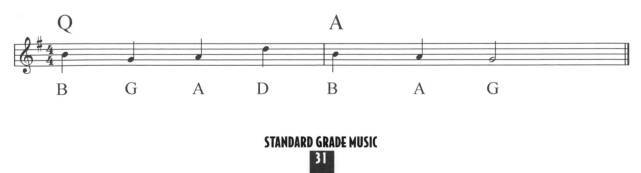

B   G   A   D   B   A   G

Make your answer simple and balanced, keeping the range of notes roughly within the notes given. Each example is in the key of G.

3. Adding a melody to given chords

You have successfully created rhythm and melody in a 'question and answer' form. Now go one step further: take a melody and a set of simple chords and attempt to improvise on them in the same 'question and answer' form. The piece *Conversations* comprises a four-bar introduction, followed by patterns of two bars of melody with chords and two bars of chords only.

In each of the two bars with chords only, you are going to improvise. Listen to the piece on CD5, following the music on page 33.

CD5 Conversations

CONVERSATIONS

You can now:

a. **play the piece as a keyboard piece, attempting to add your own melody in the empty bars**

b. **record the chords into your keyboard, and then improvise on the melody**

c. **have a friend play the accompaniment on a 'chord' instrument, while you add the melody**

d. **play your instrument along with the band on the CD**

e. **best of all, try a selection of these, varying your improvisation each time!**

Just before we start, let's consider what is going to help you create a successful improvisation:

1. **learn carefully the given part by listening to the CD a few times**

2. **keep your improvised passage in a similar style**

3. **use similar rhythms and range of notes to those given, or it will sound disjointed**

4. **think about the shape – will you use longer notes at the end of phrases – how can you make it sound finished?**

5. **enjoy it!**

Extension work

You are now going to improvise on the following melody with given chords.

ODE TO JOY

The music is written out as a melody with single finger chord names printed above the music.

Now listen to an arrangement of Beethoven's *Ode To Joy* on the CD. A further three playings of the arrangement follow without the melody. There is one bar of four beats between each playing.

CD6 Ode to Joy

Use the CD as an accompaniment or use the written chord names if you wish to play the accompaniment.

Additional tips before you begin

1. **Think of your improvising as 'talking'. You talk using groups of words to form phrases.**

2. **Listen to the chord progression. It will suggest where longer notes will be required.**

3. **Listen to the melody a few times and think how you will alter it. Here are a few ideas:**

- repeat given notes

- make first notes in the bar longer, missing out other melody notes

- miss out the first note of each bar

- add broken chords

- play the melody up or down a third at chosen places

- add in notes, e.g. the key note **G**

- introduce ornaments (quicker notes around the given melody)

Use your imagination to think up your own ideas. Keep them simple and remember you're not trying to create a completely new tune. Your first attempts may be very similar to the given melody, but you will become more ambitious!

Review Details

- Improvising – creating music spontaneously
  (usually means creating melody over
  given chords) – used extensively in jazz,
  and also in folk, rock, and world music
- Keep your improvisation within the genre
  (style) of the music
- Make sure your ideas are simple at first
- Record your work, or it may disappear for ever!
- Further help in *Writing it down* section
  on page 45

6. Words

Songwriting is another way of inventing music. As with any kind of inventing, it takes practice to become good at songwriting. Many of our greatest songwriters are self-taught, and have their own very personal way of working. There is no set magic formula for writing songs.

However, it is helpful to break down a song to see how it is constructed. You can then use some of these construction techniques to create your own songs.

Some composers add words to a given melody, while some words and music are written at the same time (simultaneously). The most common way to write a song is to add music to words that have already been written.

Choosing the lyrics

The first thing to do when writing a song, is to be very careful about the words you choose. Bear in mind the following points:

1. **Make sure you like and understand the words.**

2. **Avoid famous poems: adding music will probably not enhance them – they are famous and successful in their own right as poetry!**

3. **Read through the words carefully. Do they have a natural rhythm, a shape that is going to allow you to add a balanced melody line?**

4. **What kind of words appear in the lines? Are they going to be attractive or awkward words to sing? Do they flow with similar sounding words? For example, 'a quaint old cottage in the country' is far easier to write a melody for and sing than 'a scrap heap of rubbish propped up the derelict building'!**

5. **Read the words aloud. It's not how they look, but how they sound that matters. Look for the possibility of sequence (the same pattern of notes, repeated up or down a step), and repetition (repeating patterns of notes) where lines of words rhyme, or are similar. Sequence and repetition are good techniques to bind your melody together, making it strong and convincing.**

We have chosen these lyrics:

More Than Words Can Say

There is something in the way you say hello
Something in the way you smile
If there's one thing in this world that you should know
I couldn't leave you even for a while
In the rain and snow of winter
In my cold and darkest day
There is something in your eyes that always shines
It's more than words can ever say.

Getting an idea

Now that we have decided to use the verse from *More Than Words Can Say*, we have some very important decisions to make.

Forget about the choice of key, speed and instrumentation for the moment. It's time to experiment.

Idea >>>>>>> Develop >>>>>>>> Complete

Look again at the lyrics. You may be able to sing the first line right away. This often happens: you see the rhythm of the line, and a simple melodic pattern comes to you.

If so, play or sing these notes until you are sure you have them. Scribble them down, or tape them, as you are certain to forget them. You have an idea!

If you haven't been so lucky, that's OK. You should continue to experiment using voice or instrument – the way you doodle with a pencil – trying things out, scoring them out, trying them again. Look at the rhythm of the first line. Say the words, clap the beat.

If nothing has come yet, go to the keyboard. Create a single finger chord rhythm, fairly slow. Put together a couple of bars of chords, say D and G, four beats each. Try a simple pattern of notes that will fit the first line, either by playing or singing. It doesn't have to be a classic melody!

You now have some sort of melody line. You could work on and see where it gets you, writing a little bit down at a time.

If these efforts have not worked, a more structured approach like the one on page 39 will be of benefit to you. The lyric content suggests a fairly happy, romantic, easy-going melody. A march or a jig would not be suitable!

Working out rhythm

Let's consider the rhythm. Read the verse aloud, placing a line between the words to represent bar lines like this:

```
*              *          *    *    *      *     *    *   *
There is /  something in the way  you  / say  he- llo

     *      *       *      *    *      *        *
 / Something in the  way   you / smile
```

As you say the lyrics, accent (make louder) the underlined words as you clap (*). Look at the words which occur before the first underlined word – 'There is'. We will add **anacruses** (melody notes played before the first full bar) to them.

There are four beats between these underlined lyrics, so we will have four beats to each bar.

Using the above system, let's now add the rest of our 'beats', decide on our bar lines, and add rhythm to the lyrics.

Again, go back to saying the words aloud to decide on the particular rhythm. This should reflect the natural rhythm of the lyrics.

Take particular care to identify syllables – you will need a note for each of these. The rhythms used for syllables (and small words) are often quicker. At the end of line 4, and at the end of the verse we may wish to have longer pauses to reinforce the general shape of beginning, middle and end.

Here then is the layout we have chosen for the basic rhythm of the verse, with bar lines added.

Writing a melody

The lyrics dictate the way we construct the melody, so return to the verse to see how it has been put together.

Looking again we can see that lines 1 and 2, and lines 3 and 4 take on the simple structure of question and answer.

A statement is made (line 1), and the statement is answered (line 2) and so on. The shape of this pattern is reinforced with lines 1 and 3, and lines 2 and 4 rhyming. This is all good news for the composer!

Balanced rhyming lines create opportunities to use **sequences** and repetition.

Let's try and put some melody together, bearing these points in mind. We have experimented with a few notes beginning with D, E and F#. Let's look again at our chosen rhythm.

When we come to our first 'strong' word (in this case 'something'), we want the melody note to help to establish the key.

After experimenting with the first line lyric, we have come up with this melody phrase, suggesting the key of D major. The first 'strong' word will sound on an F#, part of the chord of D, our key chord. We will 'push' or **syncopate** some notes in the rhythm to give the song a 'natural' feel – look at the words 'say' and 'smile' – they enter *before* the start of the new bar.

Bars 3 and 4 answer bars 1 and 2, so we suggest a sequence which fits the lyrics.

Having established this part, we are now well on our way with the melody. The hardest bit is over.

Now go on and look at bars 5 to 8. We can see that the rhythm of the words is very similar to bars 1 to 4. So we can virtually repeat the musical phrase, altering it at the end to suggest the use of chord V – or 'A'. Here we have an 'E' note in the melody which is part of the 'A' chord.

If there's one thing in this world that you should know I could - n't

leave you e - ven for a while

Look now at bars 9 to 12. Something different is required here. We need to get away from the format of the first 4 lines, or the song could suddenly become a bore!

For these lines it would be wise to extend the range of the melody. After trying out several notes, a little further up the scale we have decided upon this phrase, making sure it is still in singing range:

In the rain and snow of win - ter in my

cold and dark - est day

At the end of these lines we also want to prepare the listener for a return to the melody introduced in line 1.

It would be good for lines 7 and 8 of the lyrics (on page 38) to be like lines 1 and 2. Why?
Because they are similar in word content (repetition) and we want to give the song *shape* by reintroducing the phrase we used at the beginning.

In this way we produce a balanced piece, using our chord progressions sensibly.

Adding chords

Having tried a few chords it is agreed we are in the key of D major. The range of notes we have been working around will suit the singer's voice. We are going to use the famous chord progression I, IV, and V (in the key of D major, the chords of D, G and A).

When we come to the 'halfway point' (bar 9) of our verse we do not want our piece to sound finished, so a good tip is to go to the chord of V (A in this case). The ear now expects to hear more.

We are also going to add three more chords: E minor as a substitute to G, to add interest, and B minor to give us a contrasting chord; we will also include the chord of G minor, as an interesting substitute to G before we restate the opening phrase to bring the verse to a close in the home key.

CD7 More Than Words Can Say

MORE THAN WORDS CAN SAY

John Montgomery

Use the expertise of your teacher to help you understand the many areas covered here. Remember that this is only one way of songwriting – you may have a completely different method that works for you.

As in other kinds of inventing, listen to plenty of songs, to their chords, and to their shape. You'll learn a lot by listening.

You can hear this song on CD7. Try to play it or sing it with a friend.

Extension ideas

On CD7 you heard a recording of *More than Words Can Say* for voice and keyboard.

CD8 More than Words Can Say (extended)

On CD8 we have extended the composition by:

1. **Adding an introduction. Look for a simple motif or riff (short pattern of notes which appear in the piece at various points) which you could use as an introduction. This could be a few notes which already occur in your song.**

2. **Adding an instrumental. Adding a verse of 'solo' or lead instrument and improvising over the verse chords.**

3. **Arranging. Based on your original accompaniment, create parts for guitar, bass and drums, possibly with a 'solo' instrument. Which players are available in class? This could make an interesting group performance!**

4. **Improvising. By altering the melody line rhythmically, by adding syncopation and by experimenting with chords.**

5. **Adding a harmony. Experiment with different vocal harmonies. Singing notes a third apart from the melody will often sound good.**

6. **Adding a coda (an additional passage at the end to 'round off' your song).**

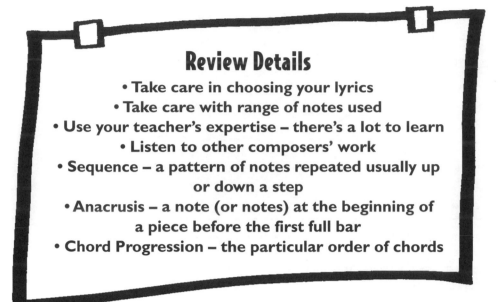

Review Details

• Take care in choosing your lyrics
• Take care with range of notes used
• Use your teacher's expertise – there's a lot to learn
• Listen to other composers' work
• Sequence – a pattern of notes repeated usually up
or down a step
• Anacrusis – a note (or notes) at the beginning of
a piece before the first full bar
• Chord Progression – the particular order of chords

Writing it down

This section offers you some help in writing your inventions down. It will help you understand the words and signs commonly used in written music.

Recordings of your inventing work on tape should match your written performance plan. If your piece is going to be recreated or performed at a later date using other players, then you have to write your instructions down in a way that they understand.

You may write your music in picture form like this:

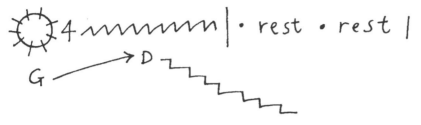

Or you may use note names with bar lines and note lengths like this:

$$\left|\frac{4}{4}\,\downarrow\;\;\downarrow\;\;\downarrow\;\;\downarrow\;\right|\!\downarrow\qquad\downarrow\qquad\left|\downarrow\;\;\downarrow\;\;\downarrow\;\;\downarrow\;\right|\,\circ\qquad\qquad\|$$

D D F D A A D D F D C

You may have your own very personal way of recording your instructions on paper – this is fine, as long as it can be understood by others.

Conventional notation

This is the system of writing down music that has been in use for hundreds of years. If you use this system, your work can be recreated and understood immediately by other players who can read music.

Here is the information you need to know to write down your music. You can refer to this when you want to write down an invention, and you can use it for instrumental parts when preparing your inventing tape.

Treble Clef (most 'smaller' instruments use this clef)

Ledger Lines

1 Octave

C (middle) D E F G A B C D E F G A B C

Note that semitones occur (marked as ⌒) between B and C, and between E and F.

Bass Clef

A B C D E F G A B C (middle)

Here is one way to help you remember the notes:

Lines (Treble Clef):

E   G   B   D   F

Every   Good   Boy   Deserves   Fun

Spaces (Treble Clef)

F   A   C   E

Lines (Bass Clef):

G   B   D   F   A

Good   Boys   Deserve   Fun   Always

Spaces (Bass Clef):

A   C   E   G

All   Cows   Eat   Grass

Rhythm and rests

Simple time:

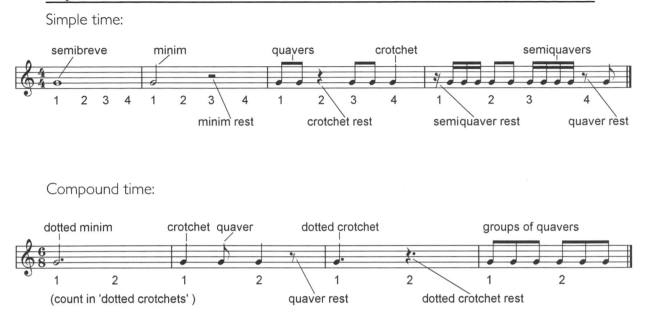

Compound time:

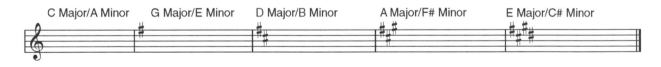

Keys

Music is written in different keys in order to obtain a particular sound, or to suit a particular instrumental range (e.g. the clarinet's). The key signature (sharps or flats at the beginning of each line of music) tells you which key the music is in. This ensures that every key uses the same system of tones and semitones.

Here are the most common keys used to write inventions in. Every major key has a relative minor key (the major key and its relative minor use the same key signature) as below:

C Major/A Minor   G Major/E Minor   D Major/B Minor   A Major/F# Minor   E Major/C# Minor

F Major/D Minor   Bb Major/G Minor   Eb Major/C Minor   Ab Major/F Minor   Db Major/Bb Minor

Chords

You can use chords to harmonise your melodies. You can play chords in different positions and you should experiment with them. Playing a chord using the same notes in a different position (or order) is called an inverted chord.

Here are the most common chords:

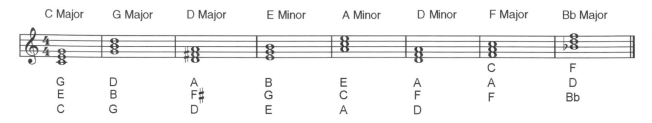

Here are the common chords you would use in the following keys:

Chords commonly used to accompany a melody in C major:

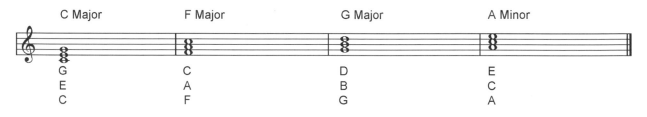

Common chords in F major:

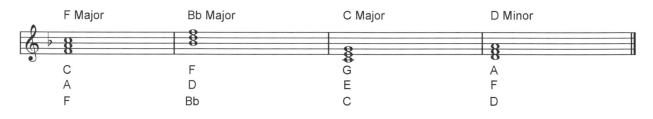

Common chords in G major:

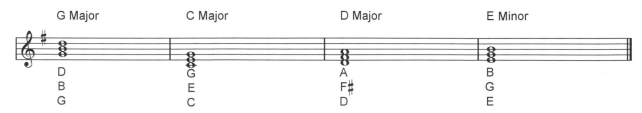

Common chords in A minor:

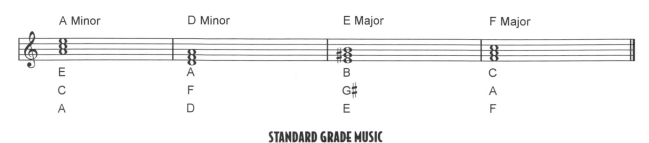

If you are playing a keyboard instrument, you could add the note name of the chord with your left hand and play the note lower down the keyboard (e.g. add the note G in the left hand with the chord of G).

Guitar and bass guitar players sometimes use a system called Tab (short for tablature). Tab is a picture of the guitar strings with the numbers written on a particular string to match the fret on the guitar. If you need an open string played, you would use the letter O, writing it on that 'string'. Here are a few notes written in notation and altered into Tab:

Melody A:

Converting notation to guitar tablature:

Melody B:

The bass guitar has only four strings and would look like this in Tab:

Guitarists also use guitar 'windows' to read chords. This time a picture of the neck of the guitar shows the strings in an upright position, with the first few frets added. Here are 8 popular guitar chords:

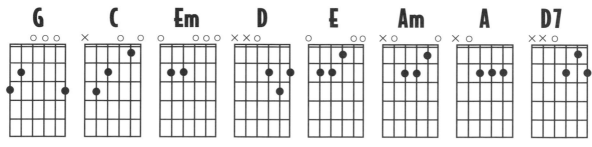

x = don't play these strings
o = play as open strings

Bb music

If you create a melody and decide that you want a clarinet or trumpet, for example, to play it, then you have to write the melody up one tone for it to sound correct. This is because these instruments are 'Bb instruments'.

Here is an example of what you would do:
Melody in key of F major:

Transposed for Bb instrument (to *sound* the same as above):

Your teacher will help you with written parts which need to be transposed.

Tempo

To state the tempo (speed) you want a piece played, you could write one of the following Italian words at the beginning of your music:

lento   (very slowly)

adagio   (slowly)

andante   (at a walking pace)

moderato   (moderately)

allegro   (quickly)

presto   (very quickly)

vivace   (fast and lively)

LISTENING

Introduction

The Listening element of Standard Grade Music gives you the opportunity to experience a wide range of musical styles. You listen carefully to live and recorded music, and discuss what you hear. The Listening element also helps you in both your Inventing and your Performing elements.

At the end of your course, you will sit one of the following:

1. **Foundation exam**   **Total time: about 45 minutes**

2. **Foundation and General exams**   **Total time: about 1 hour 30 minutes**

3. **General and Credit exams**   **Total time: about 1 hour 45 minutes**

Your teacher will advise you which will suit you best.

You will listen to several extracts from different styles of music and then answer multiple-choice questions about them. In the General and Credit exams, you will also give written answers to some questions.

This chapter includes details of the different styles of music you need to be able to recognise.

Music of Scotland

Folk songs, dances, and piping form the major part of Scotland's rich musical inheritance. They give us an insight into the lives and loves, the work and the wars that have shaped our history.

Today, Scottish folk music is enjoying an unparalleled revival, with new bands, soloists and songs constantly appearing. Sales of Scottish music and numbers attending concerts and ceilidhs (social gatherings featuring Scottish music and dance) have never been greater.

Instruments

The main instruments in traditional Scottish music are:
- **fiddle (violin)**
- **bagpipes**
- **clarsach (Scottish harp)**
- **whistle**
- **guitar**

- **Jew's-harp (ancient instrument held between the teeth, plucked by the finger)**

- **mouth organ (moothie)**

- **bodhran (hand-held drum)**

The bagpipes are also played in a Pipe Band with drums. The clarsach makes a beautiful accompaniment for singers and players, while the fiddle is often played as part of a band.

Other 'folk' instruments you will find in a typical Scottish Dance Band include:
- **accordion**

- **piano**

- **bass guitar**

- **drums**

Groupings vary, with different combinations of instruments for different compositions and occasions.

Electric instruments (e.g. guitar and keyboards) and drum kit are often included in 'contemporary' folk.

Most traditional folk music was not written down, but was passed on orally. This means that songs and tunes were heard and learnt purely by listening to them, and passed on to children and friends at home and at work.

Songs

Scottish folk songs often relate to tragic events, for example the loss of a fishing boat or a battle. Others feature the workplace. They are often very simple, for example a lullaby to rock a baby to sleep, a love song, or a song about the sea or the mountains.

Most Scottish folk songs are sung in Scots (associated with Lowland Scotland) or Gaelic (from the Highlands and Islands).

Here are five traditional types of Scottish songs:

1. Bothy Ballads – songs composed and sung mainly by farm workers who lived together for part of the year in bothies on the farm. The songs were about their work, their poor living conditions, and often about the farmer himself! Bothy Ballads were a good way for workers to find out where the best jobs, and the worst employers, were. Here is a good-humoured example of a Bothy Ballad:

CD9 The Muckin' o' Geordie's Byre

2. Waulking Songs – working songs, usually sung by women, in Gaelic. They have a very strong continuous beat to them. The songs not only relieved the boredom, but brought a sense of community and comradeship.

Listen to this example (CD10) from the island of Barra. You can clearly hear the rhythm of the cloth being beaten back and forth upon a table, and the 'question and answer' form of the music:

> ### CD10 Were you in the Mountains?

3. Mouth Music (also called Port A Beul) – a vocal performance used when no instruments were available to provide music for a dance. The words were often humorous and personal and would be improvised (made up on the spot), e.g. in CD11:

> ### CD11 Look at Ewen's Coracle

4. Scots Ballads – folk songs, often centuries old, telling a story about an important event or a disaster – for example a mining accident. The story is usually told through dialogue and narrative and can be quite long. Here is an extract (CD12) about the arrival of three gypsy lads and the effect it has on a local household:

> ### CD12 The Gypsie Laddies

5. Gaelic psalms (long tunes) – traditionally, because of the shortage of text and lack of reading skills, the psalms were sung slowly. The congregation often sounds out of time, due to the slowness of the piece and the different ways in which individuals sing it, and improvise over it. CD13 shows the unique and often very haunting effect that is created by this method of performance:

> ### CD13 Martyrs

Because instruments were not available, traditional songs are often unaccompanied.

The bagpipes

No other instrument is associated with Scotland more than the bagpipes. Its unusual 'scale' and haunting **drone** (a continuous sound which accompanies the melody) make it a unique instrument.

Over the last 600 years of Scottish history, the bagpipes have been played at royal occasions and pageantry, and were often played to encourage Scottish troops before battle. They are played at local and national events. Many towns throughout Scotland have Pipe Bands, and the tradition is as strong as ever.

Pibroch (Salutes, Gatherings and Laments, and tunes associated with historical events) is a very important part of the bagpipe repertoire.

Traditional dances

Reel – The reel is one of the oldest Scottish dances: it is fairly quick and is in ⊠ or occasionally ⊠ time. This reel (CD14) features a typical Scottish Dance Band, with the accordion playing the melody:

CD14 Sandy Cameron Reel

Waltz – The waltz came from Germany and became popular in Scotland in the 1800s. In the Scottish sense, a waltz is a collection (set) of Scottish melodies in ⊠ time, played at a moderate pace.

Jig – The jig is common to both the Irish and Scottish traditions. It is a quick dance in ⊠ or sometimes ⊠ time (compound time).

Strathspey – The Strathspey is a dance in ⊠ time and is not as fast as either the reel or the jig. It commonly uses the 'Scotch snap' rhythm, which you can clearly hear in this extract (CD15):

CD15 MacDonald of the Isles

Slow Air – a slow, simple melody in the style of a Scottish song, usually played on the fiddle or bagpipes.

Other important features of Scottish music

Scottish music is often made up using the **pentatonic** ('gap') scale. The use of **modes** (particular types of scales – neither major nor minor – but often sounding like combinations of both) is also popular in traditional melodies.

Grace notes (decorations/ornaments) also play an important part in Scottish music, especially in pibroch.

Scotch snaps (a short note on the beat followed by a longer one – ♪♩) are also a very common feature, especially in the Strathspey.

What You Should Know
- **The types of traditional instruments used in Scottish folk music**
- **The different types of Scottish songs**
- **The different types of Scottish dances**
- **How to identify grace notes**

Ragtime – Concepts at Work

Ragtime is a particular style of composition. It was very popular first in America and then in Europe in the early 1900s. This was mostly due to the young American composer Scott Joplin who wrote many Piano Rags, and made the style his own. His most famous is *The Entertainer*. Ragtime died out in the early 1920s, giving way to popular jazz.

Many people think that ragtime was an early style of jazz but as you listen to and study this piece called *Sweet Talkin' Rag*, you will realise that the two styles have little in common. Jazz is the art of improvising while ragtime is rhythmically very strict, almost march time with regular melodic lines, and occasional syncopation. The majority of ragtime compositions were written for the piano.

Follow the music of *Sweet Talkin' Rag*, while listening to the CD. Several words and phrases have been added to help you understand the meaning of the music.

Here are some features of ragtime used in *Sweet Talkin' Rag*:

- **Key G major**

- **Speed – moderato (at a moderate pace)**

- **Time signature – strictly four beats to the bar**

- **Special features – syncopation, chromatic notes, modulates briefly**

- **Form – Ternary (ABA) with a Coda**

Bar 4

Descending walking bass (a bass part which moves down in steps). This one is also in octaves (notes with same name eight notes apart).

Bars 6–8

Sequence (a group or phrase of notes repeated usually up or down one step). A good device to strengthen your inventions! Sometimes the pattern, as in this case, is not exactly the same.

Bars 14–15

Syncopation (where the natural stress or pulse has been moved).

Bars 13–15

Accent (where notes are accented or played louder than others – marked > above the accented note.)

Bars 23–25

Modulation (to suggest a new key by introducing a note or chord, not part of the key you are in (in this case note C#). This C# is, however, in the key you are suggesting (in this case D major).

Bar 34

Coda (a passage added to the end of a piece of music to give it a strong sense of ending)

Bars 36–37

Cadence (any harmonic figure, usually the combination of two chords at the end of a section or phrase). This one is a **perfect cadence** and gives a 'final' sound, using the chords of V to I.

See if you can find other bars where any of the above occur.

Check in the glossary for words mentioned in the music, but not explained above.

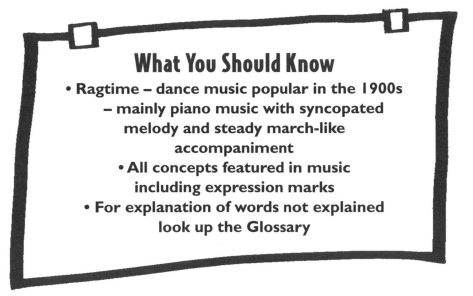

The Voice

The human voice is a musical instrument, with the added advantage of sounding words at the same time as producing notes.

A massive amount of music has been written for voice through the ages, and today the song remains the most powerful musical form. For hundreds of years the church was the central source for musical composition and performance.

By listening to music from different centuries you can identify musical progression and development. A thousand years ago a single line of music would be harmonised in parts which usually moved in parallel motion and at the octave. This was called organum. The music would be unaccompanied and in 'free rhythm', without bar lines. Often the use of melisma, or a **melismatic** effect (singing more than one, or indeed several notes on the same syllable) would be employed, for example in ancient music of Christian worship. The opposite effect, that is of always singing one note for one syllable, is called **syllabic**.

From these early forms, 'part' writing and **polyphonic** ('many-sound'/'many-voice') choral writing developed. Byrd and Palestrina, and later Bach, used polyphonic techniques to great effect in their music. **Homophonic** (parts moving together 'hymn-like', with little or no individual rhythmic interest) is the opposite of polyphonic.

Vocal compositions are often **unaccompanied**. The term used to describe unaccompanied singing in the church is '**a cappella**' ('in the chapel style').

Voice ranges

Four distinct voice ranges make up a typical mixed choir:

• **Soprano (upper female voice)**

• **Alto (lower female voice)**

• **Tenor (upper male voice)**

• **Bass (lower male voice)**

Additional voice ranges (e.g. mezzo-soprano) can also be used. 'Mezzo' means 'halfway between'. So a mezzo-soprano voice is halfway between the soprano and alto range. A counter-tenor voice has a range higher than a tenor, while a baritone has a range sitting between the tenor and bass.

The way that vocal compositions are constructed is very important. **Word setting** (the way in which the words are placed into the music, and the effect created) has a huge influence on the interpretation of both the words and the music in a particular piece. Certain other effects can be achieved, for example by using **word painting**. This is an effect which composers use to describe a passage of words in musical terms, e.g. a story about a train journey could be described by the snare drum beating out the rhythm of the train as it crosses the sleepers. More instruments are added to represent the gathering speed of the train. See the chapter on Ostinato, pages 26–28.

Oratorio

In the 1600s a musical composition called the **oratorio** was developed. An oratorio is a religious work for soloists, choir and orchestra, structured in many separate musical items, like an opera but without scenery or costumes. Oratorios would be performed in church and in concert halls. A **passion** is similar to an oratorio except it features the crucifixion of Christ as its central theme. The **cantata** is a similar composition but can also be of a secular (non-religious) nature. Here is an example from a very famous oratorio, *The Messiah* by Handel. One of the features of this music is the excellent use of **imitation** amongst the choral parts:

CD17 Hallelujah Chorus – from The Messiah (Handel)

Opera

This is a very important part of the vocal repertoire. There are several different types, but most are large compositions performed on stage using costumes and scenery. There is usually an overture (a piece of music played at the beginning by an orchestra, introducing many of the themes you hear later as songs in the opera).

There are three main types of vocal composition the composer uses to tell the story: **arias** (complete songs for soloists); **recitative** ('sung speech' used to move the story on); **chorus** (where the main body of singers perform, 'commenting on' or reinforcing the storyline).

Many famous operas have been written in Italian, by composers including Rossini, Puccini, Verdi and Mozart.

In the following aria (CD18) from a very popular Puccini opera listen to the typically simple accompaniment where the strings play the same melody line as the soprano is singing with the harp's gentle **arpeggios**. Listen to the changes in speed ('robbed time'): this is called **rubato** and is used by the composer in this typically **Romantic** work to add expression.

CD18 O Mio Babbino Caro – from Gianni Schicchi (Puccini)

Musicals

These have many similarities to operas. The story, however, is often told using the spoken word (instead of sung 'recitative') and are generally more light-hearted than opera. Musicals were first produced in twentieth-century America.

In the past twenty years the British composer Andrew Lloyd-Webber has written several worldwide smash-hit musicals including *Cats*, *Phantom of the Opera* and *Evita*. Some of the more recent musicals have abandoned the spoken word and returned to the operatic notion of recitative, e.g. *Les Miserables*.

The twentieth century has seen an explosion in popular music and song that can be traced back to African music. Different pathways have emerged. Here is a brief comment on the different styles of vocal music you need to recognise:

Jazz

Blues songs are slow, sad Afro-American compositions usually based upon the 'twelve-bar blues' chords, usually in ⊠ time.

Dixieland is a traditional style of early jazz from New Orleans around 1920, with lively, syncopated rhythms. Instruments featured are clarinets, trumpets and banjo.

Boogie-woogie is a very special kind of piano jazz. The left hand plays a repetitive and constant bass line while the right-hand melody is improvised upon. Like the blues, it is often in a twelve-bar format, but is usually played at a much faster tempo.

Swing became popular in the 1930s. Swing Bands were large and usually included saxophones. Many of the compositions have a lazy rhythmic swing to them. The singing too has a smooth laid-back sound to it, often with a gentle **syncopation** (shifting the natural accent of the music), and the use of **chromatic** notes (notes introduced in the melody/harmony outwith the key of the song).

Latin American has many of the features of jazz rhythm and harmony, often with a quick tempo and an emphasis on **percussion** (with plenty of bongos and drum patterns). Latin American songs and dances include rhumbas and sambas.

Jazz (contemporary) has become more complicated. It often shares similarities with some of today's classical music, as well as having elements of jazz's own past. Complex harmony and **cross rhythms** (e.g. 4 beats against 5) are often present.

Rock & Pop

In the 1950s teenagers found themselves with money to spend on records after the harsh years of the Second World War. Rock music developed from Rock 'n' Roll (lively three-chord song/dance music). The terms 'rock' and 'pop' cover a range of different styles now, and ever since the dance hit *Rock Around The Clock* in the late 1950s, rock and pop music has flourished.

The natural progression from Elvis Presley to The Beatles, to punk, heavy metal, reggae, house and dance means that the rock business is a massive and ever-changing industry. Here is a typical example of pop music with a little reggae flavour. Listen out for the **electronic drums** (rhythm machine) with plenty of **reverb** on the **lead vocals** and **backing vocals**:

CD19 Beautiful as You (A Montgomery)

Most rock compositions are songs. They follow a similar pattern consisting of melody with mainly 3 or 4 chords. They are usually **strophic** (the words of each verse change but the music remains the same), not **through-composed** (where the melody changes for each new verse or stanza). To add interest they may also **modulate** (change key, usually up one step), creating a climax towards the end of the song.

World Music

This term loosely covers music around the world which is not the classical or popular music of the Western/developed world.

Indian music obviously embraces everything Indian, and it is the unusual and beautiful sounds of the **sitar** that we instantly recognise. This is a complex instrument to master. It has a small body, a large neck with moveable frets and usually seven strings – with 2 of them acting as a **drone**. The sitar is often accompanied by the **tabla** – a pair of single-headed drums of different sizes.

Further east to islands such as Bali and Java, we find another fascinating sound, that of **Indonesian Gamelan**. Gamelan is the name given to the Indonesian ensemble (group) made up of percussion instruments – different-sized metallic instruments akin to our glockenspiels and metallophones. The music they play is that of a 'skeleton' melody which is developed at different tempos by different instruments and improvised by soloists. The result is a mesmerising and delightful experience where all the parts come together as one!

For rhythmical excitement and the joy of dance it is hard to equal the tantalising sounds of the **Latin percussion ensemble**. Here in South America and the Caribbean we find percussion of all shapes and forms with its roots in Afro drums and bongos. The syncopated **samba** (from Brazil) with its easy $\frac{2}{4}$ time and the rhythmical songs and dances of the **salsa** (originally from Cuba) are very infectious and an important part of everyday Latin culture. **Pan pipes** also form a distinctive part of the South American sound in countries such as Chile and Peru that border the Andes.

West Africa is reputed to be the home ground of many of our popular styles of rock, reggae and blues. Look again at the section on Blues earlier in the book, and we can see the connection – millions of West Africans were shipped to the Americas, as part of the slave trade, bringing with them their ancient rhythms. **Ghanaian drum ensembles** form an exciting part of the rich musical culture in Ghana. These groups are a real spectacle and often dance while playing their drums and percussion instruments, which include ankle and finger bells.

Here is a list of recordings if you would like to listen to the above types of music;
Indian – Ravi Shankar, *Pandit Ravi Shankar* (Ocora France)

Indonesian Gamelan – Gamelan Semar Pegulingan, *The Heavenly Orchestra of Bali* (CMP Germany)

Latin American – Elis Regina, *Essa Mulher* (Tropical Storm U.S.)
Pan pipes – Various, *Music of the Andes* (Hemisphere/EMI, UK)

Ghana – Kakraba Lobi, *The World of Kakraba Lobi* (JVC Japan)

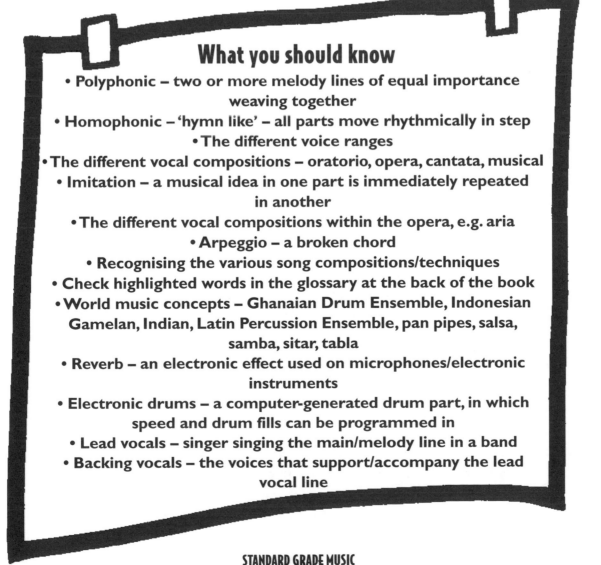

What you should know

- **Polyphonic – two or more melody lines of equal importance weaving together**
- **Homophonic – 'hymn like' – all parts move rhythmically in step**
- **The different voice ranges**
- **The different vocal compositions – oratorio, opera, cantata, musical**
- **Imitation – a musical idea in one part is immediately repeated in another**
- **The different vocal compositions within the opera, e.g. aria**
- **Arpeggio – a broken chord**
- **Recognising the various song compositions/techniques**
- **Check highlighted words in the glossary at the back of the book**
- **World music concepts – Ghanaian Drum Ensemble, Indonesian Gamelan, Indian, Latin Percussion Ensemble, pan pipes, salsa, samba, sitar, tabla**
- **Reverb – an electronic effect used on microphones/electronic instruments**
- **Electronic drums – a computer-generated drum part, in which speed and drum fills can be programmed in**
- **Lead vocals – singer singing the main/melody line in a band**
- **Backing vocals – the voices that support/accompany the lead vocal line**

Music of the 20th Century

'Music of the 20th Century' refers to the classical music of the century, and not other styles (such as jazz or rock). Hundreds of magnificent classical works have been written in the twentieth century. You'll be listening to a few of them on the CD.

Many twentieth-century composers, including Stravinsky, Bartók, Britten and Prokofiev, have not yet fully enjoyed the recognition their music deserves. Such is the way with musical composers – they are often far ahead of their time, and it takes the rest of us many more years to understand just what they are getting at!

Several concepts in your course refer to twentieth-century music and so this is a very important part of the Listening element.

In the late 1800s great change and experimentation was taking place in composing. The **Romantic** Period was drawing to a close.

Impressionism was the name given to a style of painting popular in France in the second half of the nineteenth century. Monet, Degas and other Impressionists used the textures of light and tone hinting at, rather than stating in detail, the scenes and subjects they painted.

In the same way, some composers including Debussy and Ravel tried to write music to describe a given moment suggesting, rather than constructing, large-scale thematic frameworks (like many of the earlier Romantic composers).

Whole-tone scales, **glissandi** and **chromaticism** are musical devices commonly used in the works of Debussy, as you can hear from this extract from *Prélude à l'après-midi d'un faune*. This particular piece is considered to be the 'gateway' composition to the new music of the twentieth century. Listen carefully to the way in which Debussy 'tone-paints' with the 'solo' woodwind instruments, including flute, clarinet and oboe:

CD20 Prélude à l'après-midi d'un faune (Debussy)

An important and powerful work of the twentieth century is Stravinsky's ballet *The Rite of Spring*. When it was first performed (in 1913) there was a public outcry – such were the shouts of disapproval from many members of the audience that the ballet dancers were hardly able to count to the music. This work uses many of the musical techniques which characterise the twentieth-century music that followed. In this extract listen for **discords** in the harmony, **ostinati** and **atonality**. The changing bar lengths and powerful **syncopated** rhythms and **cross-rhythms** from the orchestra give the work great originality and 'savage primitivism'. Listen also to the way in which Stravinsky uses the instruments in a **percussive** way, e.g. **col legno** (with the wood of the bow) in the string parts:

CD21 The Rite of Spring – Dance of the Young Girls (Stravinsky)

In the early 1920s, the composer Schoenberg structured his system of atonal music (music not in any key) which he had developed several years before. This system was based around the twelve notes of the scale being laid out in a particular order or 'row'. The order of notes could then be played in different ways (e.g. backwards), inverted (turned upside-down), and so on. This 'twelve-note system' became known as serialism.

Others looked to the past when composing new works. Prokofiev and Stravinsky were sometimes labelled neoclassicist because they based some of their compositions on the harmony and forms employed by earlier classical composers such as Mozart. You can hear the close reference to the classical period in this example by Prokofiev (CD 22). The orchestra scoring (similar to that used in Mozart's time) and the importance of the string section is clear. The structure of the music is heavily dependant on arpeggio and scale passages in the **minor** key, as well as repetition and sequences. The piece still creates a great sense of freedom and originality, which is one of the reasons for its popularity.

CD22 Classical Symphony No. 1 (Prokofiev)

Some composers, including Sibelius and Bartók, show a strong sense of nationalism in their music: they displayed a love for their countries and people through their compositions. In this extract from Bartók's *Music for Strings, Percussion and Celeste*, you can clearly hear a strong reference to Hungarian/Bulgarian folk music in the exciting rhythms and **syncopated** passages. This music is often **atonal**, and you can hear the use of **whole-tone** scales. Listen to the timpani and the way in which the piano is used as part of the percussion section:

CD23 Music for Strings, Percussion and Celeste (Bartók)

What you Should Know

- Impressionism
- Chromatic – scale in semitones or notes added to melody; not part of the key
- Whole tone – as in scale passage. There are no semitones, suggesting no key.
- Glissando – to 'slide' ascending or descending across the notes
- Percussion – instruments which are struck (e.g. gong, timpani, etc)
- Atonal music – music not in any key, with no 'home' key
- Tonality – opposite of atonality. Notes used in a particular established key.
- Ostinato – a constantly repeated pattern of notes
- Pedal – usually bass note sustained or repeated while harmonies change above
- Discord – notes included in chords which do not normally belong
- Romantic – a nineteenth-century style of music after Classical

Shape and Form

Like poems and paintings and books and buildings, music needs shape and form. Shape and form give compositions purpose and direction.

When you read a novel you expect it to be complete and whole. Imagine your disappointment if the storyline introduced early in the book disappeared in the middle, never to be heard of again. In music, composers use different forms and shapes to hold the listener's attention and make the music complete and whole.

You may be asked to recognise elements of form and shape in your Listening exam. You will certainly come across different forms in all the pieces you play, and you may be able to learn one or two tricks for use in your inventions.

Binary form

This is a simple form which falls into two sections (A and B). The first section often **modulates** (changes key); the second section then winds its way back to finish in the original key. A popular example of binary form is *Good King Wenceslas*.

Ternary form

This is in three distinct sections (A, B, A). The first section is repeated for the third section, with a different section (B) in the middle. A good example of this is the Beatles' song 'A Day In The Life' (on the *Sgt. Pepper's Lonely Heart Club Band* album). Look too at the Piano Rag on pages 56 and 57 – another example of ternary form.

Canon

In a **canon**, one instrument or voice sings a part and is closely imitated, note for note, by another, starting later and overlapping the first voice. You can see that, if other voices are added in this way, a very complicated composition unfolds. Canon was used to great effect by Bach in his fugues (the strictest form of contrapuntal writing). A simpler form of canon is called a round or a catch. Try singing or playing *Three Blind Mice* in parts with a few friends to get the effect. Listen to this fugue by Bach. In this composition from the **Baroque** period, you can clearly hear the 'voices' enter in imitation:

CD24 Fugue No. 16 in G minor (Bach)

Minuet and Trio

This form was popular in the classical period and is similar to ternary form. The minuet was originally a French dance with three beats to the bar. The trio was so-called because some early composers had only three instruments playing in this section rather than the orchestra. The trio eventually became known as Minuet 2, making the structure Minuet 1, Minuet 2, and Minuet 3. A good example of a Minuet and Trio is the third movement from Mozart's *Symphony No. 39 (K543)*.

Rondo

This was frequently used in the final movements of sonatas, symphonies and concertos in the classical period. It is an extension of ternary form.

The rondo form is ABACAD and so on. A is the theme. Any section which is not A is called an episode, contrasting sections in different keys. You can see that the theme (A) keeps recurring throughout the work. Mozart's *Horn Concerto No. 4* is a good example of a rondo.

CD25 Horn Concerto No. 4 – 3rd Movement (Mozart)

Symphony

A large-scale work for orchestra, usually four movements in length. Composers of symphonies include Mozart, Beethoven, Tchaikovsky, Sibelius and Mahler. A symphony is normally described by number (in the order they were written), but occasionally also by name, e.g. Tchaikovsky's *Symphony No. 6 'The Pathétique'*.

Music written in the nineteenth and twentieth centuries is often called **programme music**. This is music where the composer wishes to convey a particular mood or emotion or suggest a particular landscape, event or story.

Concerto

This word has slightly different meanings, depending on what period of music is being referred to. For the last 250 years a concerto has meant a large piece of music for soloist and orchestra. A concerto usually has three movements, the second of which is slow.

Towards the end of the first (or last) movement it is common to have a **cadenza**. This is where the solo performer improvises in the style of the work, showing off her/his skills in a great flourish of notes. Most cadenzas are now written in by the composer. Again there is a huge choice of examples spanning hundreds of years.
Here are a few world-famous concertos:

Mozart's Piano Concerto ('Elvira Madigan')

Brahms' Violin Concerto

Elgar's Cello Concerto

Listen to the different ways the string instruments are played in Brahms' Violin Concerto on the CD. You can hear the **legato** (smoothly played) melody line against the **pizzicato** string accompaniment. This music was written in the nineteenth-century Romantic period.

CD26 Violin Concerto in D Major – 1st Movement (Brahms)

...and finally

Listen to this music from 'Mars' (from the *Planets Suite*) by Holst written in the early twentieth century. This is a good example of programme music. You can hear the rhythmic **ostinato** as the heavy accompaniment to the theme, representing the huge and ugly machinery of the war which was about to ignite across Europe in 1914.

CD27 Mars – from The Planets Suite (Holst)

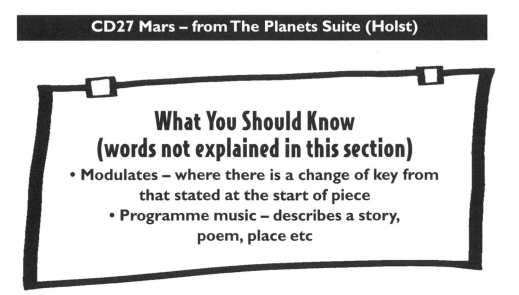

What You Should Know
(words not explained in this section)
- **Modulates – where there is a change of key from that stated at the start of piece**
- **Programme music – describes a story, poem, place etc**

Instrument File

Orchestral instruments

An orchestra is made up of four sections or families of instruments. (Instruments in brackets are not always used.)

SECTIONS	INSTRUMENTS	HOW THE SOUND IS PRODUCED
Strings	violin, viola, cello, double bass, (harp)	**Bowing and Plucking** with a bow sliding across the strings (**arco**), or plucked (**pizzicato**). They can also be played with the wood of the bow (**col legno**). Producing more than one note at a time (chords) with the bow is called **double-stopping** Producing notes by a rapid back and forth movement of the bow (sounds continuous) is called **tremolando**, creating a trembling, atmospheric effect. **Vibrato** (fast and slight fluctuation between notes) is commonly used to add expression and create a 'singing' tone.
Woodwind	flute, clarinet, oboe, bassoon, (saxophone), (piccolo)	**Blowing** using a single or double reed, except the flute and piccolo. A particular technique that wind players learn is **flutter-tonguing**, interrupting the stream of air to articulate notes (quickly repeating 'r' sounds creates the effect).
Brass	trumpet, french horn, trombone, tuba	**Blowing** using valves, except the trombone which has a slide
Percussion: Untuned	side drum, bass drum, cymbals, etc	**Striking** using different kinds of beaters or sticks, or struck together, or hit by hand
Percussion: Tuned	xylophone, timpani, glockenspiel, etc (instruments will vary depending on music)	

You can hear a selection of instruments featured on the following CD tracks:

CD3	glockenspiel	**CD23**	timpani
CD14	accordion	**CD24**	piano
CD18	harp	**CD25**	french horn
CD20	clarinet, flute, oboe	**CD26**	violin
CD21	bassoon	**CD30**	saxophone

Apart from the orchestra, there are several other instrumental groups. Here are the main ones:

Military band

Made up of a selection of woodwind instruments, brass, and percussion. CD28 is an example of a military band. (They are now often described as Concert Bands.)

CD28 The Marines Hymn/A Life on The Ocean Wave

Brass band

Unlike Military Bands, Brass Bands are made up solely of a large selection of brass instruments, with no woodwind. Cornet (similar to trumpet), flugel horn, tenor horn and baritone are commonly used. CD29 is an example of a brass band.

CD29 Tritsch-Tratsch Polka

Pipe band

Made up of bagpipes and drums (e.g. snare drums, tenor drums, bass drum).

Folk group (Scottish)

A selection of instruments (some traditional), depending on type of folk music played, including voice, fiddle (violin), clarsach (Scottish harp), acoustic guitar, whistle and accordion. Different cultures feature different instruments in their folk music, e.g. the sitar in India and the balalaika in Russia.

Jazz group

Usually features basic rhythm section of bass and drums with either piano or guitar providing chords, vocals, 'lead' instruments such as saxophone, trumpet and clarinet. The selection of instruments in the group depends on the particular style of jazz being performed. Here is a modern quartet consisting of saxophone, piano, double bass and drums (brushes). Listen to the interesting changes in rhythm and the excellent saxophone improvisations on CD30.

CD30 I Want To Talk About You (Eckstine)

Steel band

Groups of instruments made up from oil drums with their tops battered into shape to give them a particular pitch. Often used in carnivals and celebrations. Originated in the West Indies.

Rock bands/Pop bands

The difference between Rock, Pop and Soul bands is blurred today. Most still rely on **lead vocals** (singing the main melody) and **backing vocals** (voices accompanying the lead vocals), guitars, bass and drums. Sometimes variations are added to electric instruments and microphones to add **contrast** and make different **sections** of the music more interesting.

Here are some of the effects (FX) used:
Delay – the instant recording and reproduction of sounds, at chosen speeds

Reverb – an effect to change the natural acoustics of a sound. 'More reverb' means that a singer using a microphone wants to sound as if they are in a larger space (a church, for example). The acoustic effect is pleasing and appears to enhance the voice.

Distortion is an effect almost exclusively used by electric guitarists. If it's good, it should be sustained, distorted and … 'dirty'!

Apart from FX, other methods of making songs more colourful can be the variation of the instruments used. Here are some variations on the guitar:
Twelve-string guitar – this gives a rich, full sound to the chords because the strings are either doubled or doubled at the octave. **Fretless bass** brings a warm and sensitive sound to a song – listen out for plenty of glissando here. (**Slapping** the bass creates yet another effect – very rhythmical and percussive and good for 'dance music'). Even the **steel guitar** finds its way into **country** music and occasionally pop – but it is still very much associated with the Hawaiian style.

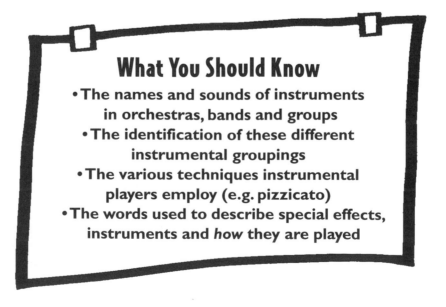

What You Should Know
- **The names and sounds of instruments in orchestras, bands and groups**
- **The identification of these different instrumental groupings**
- **The various techniques instrumental players employ (e.g. pizzicato)**
- **The words used to describe special effects, instruments and *how* they are played**

GLOSSARY OF CONCEPTS

(For further detail you should refer to a recommended music dictionary.)

'f' denotes Foundation Level concepts
'g' denotes General Level concepts
'c' denotes Credit Level concepts

c   a cappella – in the church style – usually unaccompanied choral music

g   accelerando – gradually getting faster

f   accented – make louder

f   accompany – play along with

f   accordion – a keyboard/button chord instrument popular in Scottish dance bands

f   acoustic – usually describing a non-electric instrument (e.g. acoustic guitar)

c   alberti bass – an accompanying (usually piano) bass part using the notes of a broken chord

c   aleatoric – a twentieth-century word to describe 'chance' or 'choice' in the music's composition or performance

g   alto – a low female voice

g   anacrusis – a note (or notes) played before the first beat of the bar (the upbeat)

f   answer – usually a two-bar phrase answering the first two-bar phrase (the question)

c   arco – with the bow (usually stated on music after playing pizzicato)

c   aria – a song from an opera

g   arpeggio – a broken chord

f   ascending – becoming higher in pitch

c   atonal – where the music is not in any key (used in twentieth-century music)

f   backing vocals – the voices in a modern group which accompany the lead vocal line

g   bagpipe – an instrument made up of pipes and chanter; popular in Scotland

f   band – any group of players (e.g. wind band, brass band, pop band, jazz band)

g   banjo – a stringed instrument, played like a guitar, popular in folk/country music

f   bar – a unit in which musical notes are placed. Divides the music rhythmically

c   baritone – a male voice pitched between a tenor and a bass

f   Baroque – a style of music in the early 17th to mid-18th century before the Classical period, applies to composers such as Bach and Handel

g   bass – the lowest male voice

f   bass guitar – has four strings, used to accompany other instruments; developed from double bass

f   beat – the basic unit of time used in writing and playing music

f   beats in the bar – system used to divide the music into organised units of time

g   binary – music in two distinct parts (A and B)

f   blowing – the means of producing sound on instruments such as trumpet and flute

g   blues – an important form of early jazz, developed by Afro-Americans in the USA

c   blues scale – a form of scale (similar to a combination of major and minor) used in blues music

c   boogie-woogie – jazz piano style, with repetitive rhythmical bass and improvised syncopated melody g Bothy Ballad – traditional Scottish folk songs about working conditions (usually on farms)

f bowing – drawing a bow across the strings

f brass band – group of players using instruments such as cornet, tenor horn and euphonium

f brass – name describing trombones, trumpets, french horns and tubas in the orchestra

f broken chord – notes of a chord played separately e.g. C E G (like arpeggio)

c cadence – 'resting points' that mark the end of phrases/sections; progression of two chords

c cadenza – a flourish of notes by soloist towards end of a concerto movement

g canon – strict form of writing where 2nd part imitates 1st part (before 1st part ends)

c cantata – an extended choral work for voices and usually orchestra (often religious)

f choral – relating to a choir or chorus

c chorale – congregational hymn tune of the German church (sometimes harmonised)

f chord – a combination of two or more notes played at the same time

c chorus – a large body of singers who perform together

g chromatic – moving in semitones; or, notes outside the major or minor key

c Classical – a style of music in latter 18th century. Simplicity of harmony, melodic and balanced. Applies to composers such as Mozart and Haydn.

c coda – a short section of music sometimes added at the end of a piece to 'round it off'

c col legno – striking the strings (e.g. of the violin) with the wood of the bow

g compound – the unit of a dotted crotchet beat divisible into thirds (e.g. $\frac{6}{8}$ $\frac{9}{8}$)

g concerto – a work usually in three movements for soloist and orchestra

g contrary motion – parts or notes moving in opposite directions

f contrast – used to describe changes in mood, key, speed, etc in compositions

c counter tenor – a male voice higher than tenor, similar to contralto (female)

c counter melody – a second melody part which plays above the first

c country – style of (mainly white) American folk music, e.g. 'bluegrass'. Original songs brought with settlers from Scotland and England.

g crescendo – gradually becoming louder

c cross-rhythms – different rhythmic groupings placed against each other

g delay – an electronic effect used by guitarists and on microphones to alter the acoustic sound, e.g. to make a note or phrase repeat

g descant – an additional part sung above a given melody

f descending – becoming lower in pitch

g diminuendo – gradually becoming softer

c discord – where the notes don't 'fit' harmonically (opposite of concord)

f dissonant – having discord

g distortion – an effect used by guitarists to create distorted or sustained sound

c dixieland – an early form of jazz, popular in the southern states of USA

c double-stopping – bowing more than one string at a time (on a violin, cello, etc) creating chords

g downbeat – the first strong beat in a bar

g drone – a sustained note, usually in bass, which accompanies the melody (e.g. bagpipes)

f drum fill – a flourish of drum beats to mark the end or start of musical phrases

g electronic drums – a computer device which creates drum rhythms and patterns

f ensemble – a combination of two or more performers

g fanfare – a flourish of trumpets; music often for state occasions, ceremonies

f fiddle – a violin. Called fiddle when playing in a certain style (e.g. Scottish folk music) c   flutter-tonguing – method of tonguing (rolling an 'r') used by wind players to stop/start the flow of air

f   folk group – (Scottish) group playing fiddle, accordion and whistle or other 'folk' instruments

f   folk – style of music passed down the generations through popular songs/tunes

c   fretless bass – a bass guitar with no frets creating a sound similar to a double bass. Listen out for sliding notes (glissandi)

g   Gaelic Psalms – 'long tunes', i.e. improvised songs of worship with 'leader' and congregation, which are sung in Gaelic (usually in the Western Isles)

g   gamelan music – percussion players create melody (skeleton), using different sized 'metallophones' to decorate and develop a piece as one 'complete' sound (associated with Indonesia)

g   Ghanaian drum ensemble – groups/tribes from Ghana playing elaborate and exciting dance rhythms on percussion instruments, shakers and finger/ankle bells

c   glissando – to 'slide' through the notes in an ascending or descending 'scale'

c   grace notes – additional notes added to decorate a melody

c   ground bass – a repeated phrase or motif heard in the bass part

f   guitar – popular instrument with 6 (or 12) strings which are strummed or plucked

f   harmony – the sounding of two or more notes together

g   harp/clarsach – a plucked string instrument. Clarsach used in Scottish folk music

c   homophonic – having many sounds (harmony) which move rhythmically as one, in step

c   hymn – religious song usually sung by congregation in church

g   imitation – where one theme or statement in one part is immediately imitated in another part

c   imperfect cadence – 2 chords creating 'resting point' in music, e.g. chord I to chord V. This sounds unfinished.

c   Impressionism – style of music in France (late 1800s). Mood of music suggested rather than stated.

g   improvise – make up, compose 'on the spot'

c   Indian – describing music from India, e.g. sitar music

g   Indonesian gamelan ensemble – an ensemble (group) from Indonesia of gongs, 'metallophones' and drums, usually 15–20 players

c   inverted pedal – upper part sustained or repeated while harmonies change below

c   interval – the distance between 2 notes, e.g. C to G is a fifth; C to E is a third

f   jazz – a style of music which originated from Black Americans in the 19th century

f   jazz group – consists of instruments such as piano, bass, drums, guitar, clarinet, trumpet

g   jig – a quick dance usually in $\frac{6}{8}$ time. Popular in Scottish and Irish folk music

f   keyboard – any instrument which uses a set of keys (e.g. piano, synthesiser, organ)

f   Latin American – a style of jazz dance music from South America

g   Latin Percussion ensemble – drums/percussion group prominent in rhythmical Latin dance music

f   lead vocals – singer of the main line/melody of a song. Usually part of a modern band, e.g. a pop band, jazz band.

f   leaping melody – a melody which jumps about as opposed to one which moves in steps

f   legato – smoothly, without breaks in the sound

g   major – a particular pattern of notes making up a key, chord or scale

f   march – a composition used for marching, usually in strict $\frac{2}{4}$ or $\frac{4}{4}$ time

c   melismatic – effect where lyrics or words use more than 1 note per syllable, e.g. plainsong

c   mezzo-soprano – a female voice between a soprano and alto voice

c minimalist – late twentieth-century style where simple patterns/ostinati are developed, extended and added to each time they are repeated

g minor – a particular pattern of notes which applies to key, chords and scales

g minuet and trio – a musical form popular in the Classical period (ABA)

c modal scale – a scale of music, not major or minor, originally used in medieval music

c modulation – a change of key from that already established

g mouth music (port a beul) – a kind of vocal improvisation used to accompany Scottish dance

g musical – like an opera, but often more light-hearted and usually with spoken dialogue

c muted – dampened, quietened (referring to the sound of an instrument)

g note-cluster – twentieth-century term to describe 'chord' of several adjacent notes played together

c obbligato – an instrumental accompaniment part that is compulsory to the music

f octave – an interval of 8 notes, having the same letter names, e.g. C – C

f off the beat – where the accent is on the weak beat – as in syncopation

g opera – a play that is sung and uses costumes and scenery

c oratorio – music for soloists, choir and orchestra with a religious theme, in many sections

f orchestra – a large group of musicians made up of woodwind, strings, brass and percussion

f organ – a keyboard instrument (of various sizes), often with foot pedals and pipes

g ornament – additional notes (e.g. trills or turns), added to a given passage to enhance it

f ostinato – a short pattern of notes constantly repeated

g pan pipes – graded sets of pipes bound together which you blow across. Often associated with Andean South America (Peru, Chile, etc)

c passing note – a note passing from one harmonic chord to the next, usually in steps

c Passion – large work for orchestra, soloists and chorus, like an oratorio. Story of crucifixion of Christ.

f pattern – the description given to a particular rhythm or sequence of notes, e.g. an ostinato

c pedal – a note sustained or repeated in the bass part while the harmonies above change

g pentatonic scale – a scale made up of a pattern of five different notes

f percussion – instruments which produce their sound mainly by being struck

c perfect cadence – 2 chords creating a 'resting point' in music, e.g. chord V to chord I. This sounds final and complete.

f phrase – a group of notes expressed as one statement, as in language

c pibroch – a type of Highland bagpipe music – often very elaborate

f pipe band – a Scottish marching band made up of bagpipes and drums

f pipes – shortened version of the names of instruments such as bagpipes, pan pipes

c pizzicato – the plucking of stringed instruments, as opposed to using the bow

f plucking – pulling the strings with the fingers (pizzicato)

c polyphonic – having 'many sounds', with several voices or instruments combined contrapuntally

f pop – a style of modern music, usually songs, associated with 'youth culture'

f pop group – a modern group who usually sing and play electric guitars and drums

g programme music – music which describes a scene, a story or emotions

f pulse – beat

g ragtime – a style of lively music (usually for piano) popular in the USA, featuring syncopation

g rallentando – a direction to slow down

c recitative – sung speech in opera often used to move the plot or story on

g   recorder – an early form of woodwind instrument, now popular in schools

f   reel – a Scottish (or Irish) dance in quick but smooth four time

c   register – a group of notes belonging to a particular pitch range

c   relative major – major key that shares same key signature as minor, e.g. G major and E minor. Connected through modulation.

c   relative minor – minor key that shares same key signature as major, e.g. D minor and F major. Connected through modulation.

f   repetition – a passage or pattern of notes which are repeated

g   reverb – an effect similar to 'delay' used in amplified instruments or microphones to promote changes in acoustics, e.g. music played in a room can sound as if played in a large hall

f   riff – a short phrase, repeated frequently throughout (often used in pop and jazz)

f   rock – a style of modern popular music with roots in rock 'n' roll

f   rock group – a modern band usually with singer, electric guitars and drums

f   rock 'n' roll – a style of dance music popular in the 1950s, from the USA

g   Romantic – a style of music from the 19th century. Rich in harmony and very melodic. Includes music by composers such as Tchaikovsky and Wagner.

g   rondo – a composition in which the theme (A) keeps recurring (e.g. ABACADA...)

f   round – where the theme is started and repeated in a staggered fashion throughout parts

g   rubato – 'robbed time' – changes in tempo to create expression

g   samba – heavily syncopated Brazilian dance music, with an easy $\frac{2}{4}$ beat

g   salsa – rhythmical song/dance music from Cuba/Carribbean

g   scale – a passage of notes moving up or down in steps

c   scherzo – a lively movement from a symphony or sonata usually in $\frac{3}{4}$ time

f   Scotch snap – a short note on the beat followed by a longer one ♪♩.

g   Scots Ballad – a Scottish folk song, often describing a disaster; a story told through song

f   Scottish dance band – a band made up of fiddle, accordion, piano and drums

f   section – usually a particular part of a piece of music, e.g. the 'middle' section; or, a part of the orchestra, e.g. the brass section

g   semitone – a half tone or half step from one note to the next, e.g. F# to G

f   sequence – a pattern of notes usually repeated up or down one step

f   simple time – crochet beats divisible into halves (e.g. $\frac{2}{4}$, $\frac{3}{4}$, $\frac{4}{4}$ time)

c   sitar – a guitar-like instrument from India with a long neck and usually 7 strings. It has a very distinctive sound.

f   slapping – a word used to describe a method of playing the bass guitar – to 'slap' the strings

c   slide guitar – stringed instrument played on a stand using a 'bottle neck' on finger. Listen out for sliding effect, e.g. as in Hawaiian music.

g   slow air – a simple melody in the style of a slow Scottish song, usually played on the fiddle or bagpipes

f   solo – a piece or passage performed by one player or singer

g   soprano – a high female voice

c   soul – a style of popular music, black American roots, emotional. Comes from gospel and blues.

f   staccato – short detached notes

f   steel band – a group using oil drum tops, tuned to different pitches (from the West Indies)

f   stepwise – melody which moves about in steps (as opposed to jumps) f   Strathspey – a traditional Scottish dance in $\frac{4}{4}$ time played at a moderate speed (features Scotch snap)

f   striking – hitting an instrument (usually percussion) in order to create a particular sound

f   strings – orchestral family of instruments including violin, viola, cello and double bass

c   strophic – in song, where the lyrics in each verse change but the music remains the same

f   strumming – a means of producing sound on instruments such as guitar and banjo

c   suspension – a kind of discord, where one note is held over from previous chord

f   sustained – where sounds are held on

g   swing – a popular style of dance music created in the 1930s (Big Band)

c   syllabic – where each syllable of a word is given a note (opposite of melismatic)

g   symphony – a large-scale orchestral work usually in four movements

g   syncopation – where the natural pulse has been shifted onto the weaker beat

c   tabla – a pair of Indian drums often used to accompany the sitar

g   tenor – a high male voice

g   ternary – a composition in three parts: (A) first part (B) a new second part (A) first part

g   theme – the main melody of a piece of music

g   theme and variation – where the theme is stated and then altered (e.g in speed, key, style, instruments)

c   through-composed – where the music changes for each stanza/verse

c   tierce de picardie – to end a piece of music written in a minor key with the chord of the major key of the same name. For example a piece in key of G minor ends with the chord of G major.

c   tonal music – music where the key note or tonic is established (as opposed to atonal music)

c   tremolando/tremolo – rapid movement of the bow creating a trembling effect

c   trill – ornament in which two consecutive notes are played alternately and quickly

c   twelve-string guitar – an acoustic guitar with 12 strings, tuning as 6 string, except strings doubled or doubled at the octave

f   unaccompanied – with no instruments accompanying or playing along with

f   unison – where all parts play or sing the same notes, (as opposed to harmony)

g   upbeat – the last beat of a bar (before the first downbeat of next bar)

g   vamp – improvise simple chords (usually on the piano) to accompany a tune

c   vibrato – an effect meaning fast fluctuations between notes. Used by singers and string players to improve expression and feeling.

f   vocal – using the voice

g   walking bass – a jazz bass part which uses mainly scale passages, pinning down the beat

g   Waulking Song – a traditional Scottish song performed during repetitive work (Gaelic)

f   waltz – a popular dance composition in $\frac{3}{4}$ time, at a moderate pace

c   whole-tone – a whole-tone scale has no semitones, popular in some twentieth-century music

f   wind/military band – band made up of woodwind, brass and percussion

f   woodwind – a section of the orchestra, mainly flutes, clarinets, oboes and bassoons

c   word painting – using music to describe words, e.g. 'here comes the rain' – instruments play short sharp sounds, increasing in volume and speed

c   word setting – the setting of words to music in a particular musical framework

LIST OF CD TRACKS

All tracks composed and/or performed by John Montgomery unless stated otherwise.

CD No.	Title	Composer	Performer	Recording Co.	Page
CD1	Highland Walk			Leckie & Leckie	16
CD2	Carolina Blues			Leckie & Leckie	20
CD3	Raining on Loch Lomond			Leckie & Leckie	25
CD4	From a Railway Carriage			Leckie & Leckie	29
CD5	Conversations			Leckie & Leckie	32
CD6	Ode to Joy	Beethoven		Leckie & Leckie	35
CD7	More than Words Can Say 1		vocals Brian Carty	Leckie & Leckie	42
CD8	More than Words Can Say 2		vocals Brian Carty	Leckie & Leckie	43
CD9	The Muckin' o' Geordie's Byre (Bothy Ballads)	(traditional)	Jimmy MacBeath (No. CDTRAX 9001)	Greentrax Records	53
CD10	Were you in the Mountains? (Waulking Songs from Barra)	(traditional)	Mary Morrison (No. CDTRAX 9003)	Greentrax Records	54
CD11	Look at Ewen's Coracle (Music from the Western Isles)	(traditional)	Annie Arnott (No. CDTRAX 9002)	Greentrax Records	54
CD12	The Gypsie Laddies (Music from the Western Isles)	(traditional)	Jeannie Robertson (No. CDTRAX 9005)	Greentrax Records	54
CD13	Martyrs (Gaelic Psalms from Lewis)	(traditional)	Alasdair Graham & Congregation (No. CDTRAX 9006)	Greentrax Records	54
CD14	Sandy Cameron (Fiddler and his Art)	Scott Skinner	Donald McDonell (No. CDTRAX 9009)	Greentrax Records	55
CD15	MacDonald of the Isles	(traditional)	Colin Dewar	Greentrax Records	55
CD16	Sweet Talkin' Rag			Leckie & Leckie	56
CD17	Hallelujah Chorus (The Messiah)	Handel	Acad. & Chorus St Martins (No. 444 824-2, P7925)	Decca	60

CD No.	Title	Composer	Performer	Recording Co.	Page
CD18	O Mio Babbino Caro (from Gianni Schicchi)	Puccini	Lesley Garrett/ Philharmonia Orch. (No. PCD 2709)	Telstar Records	61
CD19	Beautiful as you	Andy Montgomery		Leckie & Leckie	62
CD20	Prélude à l'après-midi d'un faune	Debussy	London Symphony Orchestra (No. 455152-2)	Decca	64
CD21	The Rite of Spring	Stravinsky	L'Orchestre de la Suisse Romande (No. 443467-2)	Decca	65
CD22	Classical Symphony No. 1 Gavotta	Prokofiev	Orpheus Chamber Orchestra (No. 423 624-2)	Deutsche Grammophon	65
CD23	Music for Strings, Percussion and Celeste	Bartók	Boston Symphony Orchestra (No. 439 402-2)	Deutsche Grammophon	65
CD24	Fugue No. 16 (G minor) (The Well Tempered Clavier)	Bach		Leckie & Leckie	67
CD25	Horn Concerto No. 4 (K495) (3rd Movement)	Mozart	Peter Bann/ASMIF (No. 426 207-2 Vol 2)	Philips Classic Productions	68
CD26	Violin Concerto in D major (1st Movement)	Brahms	Joshua Bell/ Cleveland Symphony Orchestra (No. 444 811-2 PY925)	Decca	68
CD27	Mars – from The Planets Suite	Holst	Royal Philharmonic Conducted by Vermon Handley (No. TRP 007)	Tring International	69
CD28	A Life on the Ocean Wave	Russell	Royal Marines	Grasmere Records	71
CD29	Tritsch-Tratsch Polka	Strauss	Williams-Pairey Engin. Band (No. STCD242)	Grasmere Records	71
CD30	I want to talk about you	Eckstine	John Coltrane (No. ST9647, STCD 248)	Charly Schallplatten	71